JAY BERRY'S SPORTS ODYSSEY AND BEYOND

To Leonard,

An accounting of my past, at least as accurately as I remember it.

Hope you enjoy!

Jay

JAY BERRY'S SPORTS ODYSSEY AND BEYOND

FROM TURF TO TELEVISION & THE BLACK 14 PROTEST

◆ ◆ ◆

Jerome (Jay) Berry

Copyright © 2019 Jerome (Jay) Berry
All rights reserved. This book or any portion thereof may not be reproduced or used in any manner whatsoever without the express written permission of the publisher except for the use of brief quotations in a book review.

ISBN-13: 9781073733507

So, whether you eat or drink, or whatever you do, do all to the glory of God.

1 Corinthians (10:31) English Standard Version (ESV)

Forward
RICKEY HAMPTON

When I first learned about the Black 14 incident, I was stunned to see my friend Jay Berry was part of the group. Fourteen young Black men, members of the 1969 University of Wyoming football team, were kicked off the squad by Head Coach Lloyd Eaton for asking to wear armbands in an upcoming game against Brigham Young University – a year after Tommie Smith and John Carlos raised their black-gloved fists and long before Colin Kaepernick took a knee. Jay was called Jerry Berry at the time and was a standout safety.

I have known Jay for more than 30 years. I knew him as a fellow sports journalist and admired him for his brilliant reporting for WXYZ in Detroit. I have spent many hours with Jay, traveling around the country to sporting events, and we discussed many topics.

Never did he mention that he was part of the 'Wyoming Black 14.' In retrospect, I shouldn't have been surprised considering what a humble and down to earth person that Jay is. Jay never boasted. He just came to work and did his job superbly.

My admiration for Jay is at an entirely new level upon hearing his story of the 'Wyoming Black 14'. The courage it took for Jay and his teammates to stand up for what they believed is right, to withstand the pressure from the school, and the rejection by many in the state that supported Eaton, is a testament to their resolve and perseverance.

Jay Berry

Jay was always a magnificent storyteller during his award-winning career. Now he is telling us arguably the most important story of his life, the story of the 'Wyoming Black 14'.

(Rickey Hampton was an award-winning sports columnist for the Flint Journal and Booth Newspapers in Michigan.)

Table of Contents

	Introduction: In Fifty Years, What Has Changed?······xi	
Chapter 1	Who Are We? Who Am I?························1	
Chapter 2	A Child - Then a Man, With Little In Between ········11	
Chapter 3	"...How They Run—Yes Run—When They Hear Him Come..."·································31	
Chapter 4	If First You Don't Succeed…····················47	
Chapter 5	Turn Your TV On T-Town!······················65	
Chapter 6	Hangin' in Houston·························81	
Chapter 7	State Street...That Great Street················99	
Chapter 8	Motown - My Kind of Town ···················111	
Chapter 9	Wanted – A Michigan Man!····················155	
Chapter 10	Barry, The Hitman, and The Queen ··············181	
Chapter 11	Life Through My Rear View Mirror...With the Head Beams Focused on God ·····················201	
Chapter 12	The Black 14 - The Lies, Like the Story, Will Not Die · 209	
	Acknowledgements ························215	

INTRODUCTION
In Fifty Years, What Has Changed?

KNEEL OR NOT? FIVE DECADES Before Colin Kaepernick, A Black Armband Protest Still Remains Relevant.

September 20th 1969, Laramie, Wyoming. The sun rises over the mountains and brushes past the pines with the bravado of bison roaming the plains. No complaints coming from War Memorial Stadium where the Cowboys are opening a new college football season. The stands are ablaze with vibrant colors, as bands from across the state get ready to help usher in Wyoming's equivalent of the Mardi Gras. Ragtime Cowboy Joe is being sung with the intensity you would expect from a rowdy bunch of 'pokes invading town, some from as far away as Yellowstone, 400 miles to the Northwest. It's a big state, matched only by the expectations of the faithful sporting Wyoming's Brown and Gold colors.

This last year I have grown to embrace the uniform highlighted by the polished sun-colored pants and the number 21 is the same one I wore in high school. It became a must have a couple of years ago, when Jim Kiick, a future NFL star, wore it while leading Wyoming to a closely contested Sugar Bowl showdown with LSU. Then there is the helmet with the bucking cowboy. It is one of the most popular in all of college football. I know playing as good as I think I look will not be easy. The Cowboys have put together three straight Western Athletic Conference titles. But Arizona, the opponent today, handed Wyoming its only loss in the league the previous year. Enter yours truly, an unproven starting sophomore safety from Tulsa, Oklahoma.

It's a surreal feeling. I'm living a dream. The culmination of seven years of preparation. Two years ago I was celebrating the Oklahoma AAA state high school football championship. A year ago I was a member of Wyoming's undefeated freshman team. But this is the BIG TIME, played out before a regional televised audience throughout the mountain west. Every mistake or highlight has the chance to make it back home. I want to show progress and also have some questions answered, like am I good enough? What can I say...I had the game of my life!

But inside of a month the unbelievable joy and notoriety I experienced was long gone. The players, the coach, the school, the state... even the governor were caught up in a racially infused controversy that will eventually drop the fast charging Cowboys from the ranks of the undefeated...and devastate the football program for years. It was known as The Black 14 incident. 50 years later it is still a stain the university can't wash away, the players can't forget, and a nation...most of it, can't believe!

Freedom of speech and the right to peacefully protest was at the heart of our controversy and it remains today. Free speech is a privilege, says our Constitution, but try convincing Colin Kaepernick of that. The National Football League quarterback became an outcast or hero, depending on your opinion of his protest, following the numerous murders of unarmed Black men throughout America. In 2016 he started taking a knee during the playing of the national anthem prior to games and soon found himself out of a job and the scourge of millions. He isn't the first to encounter the wrath of disapproving Americans and won't be the last. Slavery, women's suffrage, civil rights...and many other causes have introduced us to numerous courageous individuals who have fought to make this country a better place and force it to live up to its constitutional commitments.

In March of 2017, Kaepernick became a free agent and apparently too hot to handle. No team would touch him. President Donald Trump joined the fray, calling for players to be fired or suspended for failing to stand for the national anthem. Even Jim Brown, a longtime civil rights advocate and member of the Pro Football Hall of Fame, was quoted as saying, that while "he wants to be in [Kaepernick's] corner," he would never "desecrate my flag and my national anthem." On the flip-side, the quarterback received numerous honors because of his position against racial injustice, including the 2017 Sports Illustrated Muhammad Ali Legacy Award.

Kaepernick filed a grievance against the NFL in November of 2017, alleging the owners colluded to keep him out of the league. The following summer, arbitrator Stephen Burbank ruled in favor of Kaepernick and allowed his case against the NFL to go forward. Safety Eric Reid, Kaepernick's former teammate with the San Francisco 49ers, who joined the quarterback by kneeling during the playing of the National Anthem, also filed a collusion grievance against the NFL in May of 2018.

Kaepernick's saga contained a profitable twist when Nike, the multi-billion dollar incorporation that specializes in athletic apparel, made him the face of its 30th anniversary "Just Do It" advertising campaign. Within weeks of its release, Nike's stock reflected a five percent increase, equaling six billion dollars in gains. This, after an early reaction by some customers who resorted to burning their shoes in protest. Many hadn't even seen the commercial, which carried a positive message of physical and mental empowerment. By late September 2018, some San Francisco 49er fans were pleading for the return of Kaepernick after Jimmy Garoppolo suffered a season-ending knee injury.

In February of 2019, both Kaepernick and Reid settled their cases with the NFL. No details were revealed as both the player and the League cited a confidentiality agreement as part of the resolution.

CHAPTER 1

Who Are We? Who Am I?

I AM A PROUD AMERICAN, with as many inalienable rights to be here… as anyone. Cut me open and I bleed Red, White, Blue, Black, Brown and every color in between. But even our young children realize that we are a work in progress. They might not put it that way, but if they could…they probably would. America has been evolving since before its declared independence from England. Every step a struggle, sometimes sprinkled with immediate success…but often followed by failure, decades of stagnation and immobility. Yet, we essentially want the same things: the ability to provide for us and our families, a safe place to live, health insurance, an education…and to be treated fairly. However reaching these aspired goals come at a price, which has been painfully reflected through America's turbulent past and continues today.

Life doesn't always present us with choices. Sometimes they are made for us…and we are left to deal with the consequences. How we are perceived and labeled…our very existence has in many cases, been basically taken away from us. Unfair? Absolutely! One of the frustrating things for me has been trying to set straight what turned into the Black 14 incident, once and for all.

How can any sane person justify destroying a major college football program, when it's ascending up the rankings and enjoying an undefeated season? Everything that has been painstakingly achieved is trashed. Oddly, history might show that Brigham Young University, the institution targeted in our firestorm, may have benefited the most.

Wednesday, October 15th, 1969. While in the midst of completing a week of preparation for BYU, I started hearing some locker room chatter about last year's game at Provo. Wyoming won the game in exciting fashion...but while leaving the field, some Black players complained that the sprinklers had quickly been turned on to cleanse it, because Blacks had competed on it. I couldn't believe what I was hearing. It made no sense! I felt as if I had been thrown back in time. I questioned the legitimacy of what I was being told and wondered what it had to do with us. What follows is what I learned.

BYU is completely owned by The Church of Latter-Day Saints (LDS or Mormon Church) and run under the auspices of its Church Educational System. The Church was established in 1830, during an era of great racial division in the United States. During the first two decades of the Church's existence, a few Black men were ordained to the priesthood. But after the death of Joseph Smith, the founder of Mormonism and the Latter-Day Saints movement, that changed. In 1852, Brigham Young, the second president of the LDS Church, publicly announced that men of Black African descent could no longer be ordained to the priesthood. When Brigham Young died, presidents who followed restricted Blacks from receiving the temple endowment or being married in the temple. There would be different theories by Church leaders and members to explain the priesthood and temple restrictions. But none are accepted today as the official doctrine of the Church, according to the Church hierarchy.

It was believed by a lot of Whites, especially those who migrated West from the South and who owned slaves, that Blacks were inferior. This helped to initiate the changes by the Church toward Blacks. In addition, we were also thought to be descendants from the biblical Cain, who killed his brother Abel...and then was cursed by Black skin.

This is what was alluded to by the Black players, who brought up the cleansing of the ground in Provo. Some also took exception to the name-calling that had racial undertones...and what was perceived as dirty plays.

On campus, The Black Students Alliance (BSA) announced its intention to stage a non-violent demonstration Saturday, outside War Memorial stadium, before the BYU game. Thus, the BSA joined other universities in the West, and in particular in the Western Athletic Conference (WAC), who were protesting BYU's policies towards Blacks.

At the time, the Black Student Alliance distributed the following material:

Why we must Protest

Our position is that a practice and interpretation clearly racist, is no less so because it is couched in religious terms.

Our Humanity Demands

1. That University Officials at Wyoming, as well as other schools in the Western Athletic Conference, not use student monies and university facilities to play host to thereby, in part, sanction those inhuman and racist policies of the Church of Jesus Christ of Latter Day Saints, (LDS).
2. That all athletic directors in WAC, out of regard for the humanity of their Black Athletes, refuse to schedule and play games with BYU so long as the LDS Church continues such policies as outlined above.
3. That all Black athletes in WAC protest in some way any contest with BYU so long as the LDS Church continues such policies.
4. That all people of good will—whatever their color—athletes included, protest along with their Black fellows, a policy of the

LDS Church clearly racist and inhuman. The symbol of this protest is the black armband worn during each contest with a BYU team.

This hit me, and I'm sure some others, like a bolt of lightning! I never saw this coming. Sure there were some players who expressed their feelings regarding last year's BYU game in Provo. But this? I was focused on our season and school...and since I was no longer living in the dorms, I wasn't aware of any talk about demonstrations in Laramie or elsewhere in the Western Athletic Conference.

We, the Black players, met Thursday and felt a meeting with our no-nonsense Head Coach, Lloyd Eaton, was needed...and quickly. It was decided our tri-captain, Joe Williams, would see if this was possible. Joe talked to Eaton, and told him of some concerns we had. Joe returned and said Eaton warned us about wearing black armbands during the game Saturday. We asked Joe to reach out to the coach again, so we could express ourselves to him in person. A Friday morning meeting was set up at the fieldhouse.

During my year-and-a-half in Laramie, I had little direct contact with Eaton. But surely he would be a reasonable person and hear what we had to say, I thought. Whatever we wanted, armbands or another means of protest, or nothing at all...we knew he had the last word. There would be no demands or threats of a walkout...or anything like that. But we hoped to tell him, face-to-face, things that were troubling us. Basically I wanted to ask some questions. What's wrong with that? So Friday came...and while walking over to meet with our coach, I asked Tony McGee, who had played varsity the previous year...what he thought would happen in the meeting. He turned and gave me a serious look before saying, "I think we're going to lose our scholarships, our jobs." I said, really? He said, "Really!" Now my mind was really racing. This is all crazy! Can't even talk to the coach? Unfortunately and regrettably, Tony was right! Oh yeah, we were wearing black armbands.

But this was not Saturday, and we weren't in team uniforms. We were students and we weren't marching. As for the armbands, each player had his own reason for putting one on. For me, it was about showing solidarity in addressing some issues at Wyoming: treatment by some coaches, professors and social situations. We had never discussed these things with those in power. Mormon's? I didn't even know what a Mormon was before arriving in Laramie. In fact, Wally Stock, one of my favorites on the freshman team, was a Mormon. He invited me to spend Christmas with his family. I seriously considered it, but was too homesick to accept.

When we entered the fieldhouse, we were escorted to the seats and were told Eaton would be with us shortly. The mood was somber, impending doom was what I was feeling. Our head coach showed up with a couple of assistants and before we had a chance to open our mouths, Eaton told us, "I can save you a lot of time, from this moment on, you'll never play another down of football for the University of Wyoming. Were it not for me, you would be at Grambling or Morgan State (traditional Black colleges) or on Negro or Colored relief (welfare) somewhere starving to death. Most of you come from broken homes and don't even know who your fathers are." Every time we tried to say something, we were told to "shut-up!"

What was seen by some as racial issues with BYU, was nothing like we had been hit with by OUR OWN HEAD COACH! On top of that… we were kicked off the team without having a chance to ask a single question! At one point I looked around and saw that defensive coordinator, Fritz Shurmur, had tears in his eyes. I knew there would be no going back. Ann Marie Walthall, the wife of a faculty member, happened to be walking in the fieldhouse below us. She would later be quoted as saying, "The coach insulted the players in an angry manner, which further polarized the situation. It was pretty belligerent talk, I felt embarrassed for the young men hearing this tirade."

As college athletes we usually knew our opponents and their capabilities, but when we faced U.S. District Court Judge Ewing T. Kerr, the state of Wyoming, it's governor Stanley Hathaway, Lloyd Eaton, the head football coach of Wyoming's only four year university, it's President William Carlson, Athletic Director Red Jacoby and the board of trustees...they gave a new meaning to home field advantage.

I was in a fog...stunned, shocked and wondered what my next step would be. Everything – I mean everything I had worked towards achieving over half my life – gone in a flash of anger! I couldn't make sense of it. 12th in the country and undefeated! Now? Those emotions were echoed by the other 13. We asked for and received a meeting with the President of the University of Wyoming, William Carlson. We also requested that Coach Eaton be present. As we headed over to President Carlson's office at Old Main, we heard that it was being broadcast we had quit the team. The lies had already started...and they were being spread with unbelievable speed!

President Carlson was joined by Athletic Director Red Jacoby and student leaders. Eaton was a no-show. Jacoby wasn't even in our meeting with Eaton earlier. It became abundantly clear who was running the show...and it wasn't the Athletic Director. Another meeting later that evening would include Carlson, The Wyoming Board of Trustees, and Wyoming Governor, Stanley K. Hathaway, who came from Cheyenne in heavy snow, 50 miles away ...but no Eaton. We thought his popularity and power knew no bounds in the state and this confirmed it. He couldn't and wouldn't be made to show. It was a marathon session, lasting about seven hours and not ending until after 3:00 am Saturday morning. The game was just hours away. Before leaving, the governor raised the question, "What would it take for you to go back on the team?" What? We didn't leave the team, we were kicked off! "Fire the coach!" came a reply out of nowhere, by one of the Black players. This hadn't been discussed or considered! However, following that response, the governor turned and walked away, with nothing else to say.

That remark would haunt us when the university mounted its defense. The trustees confirmed our dismissal. "The players will not play in today's game or any during the balance of the season"...so says a press release. In addition, it reads "The dismissals result from a violation of a football coaching rule Friday morning."

Jacoby further noted in the release, "Ample notice was given to all members of the football team regarding rules and regulations of the squad, some of which cover a ban on participation in student demonstrations of any kind. Our football coaching staff has made it perfectly clear to all members of the team that groups, or factions, will not be tolerated and that team members will be treated as individuals."

If that were true, why didn't the governor ask us individually, what it would take for us to go back on the team? This was an absurd question to begin with. Again, we didn't fire ourselves! As for the so called coaches' rule, this was the first I had heard of it. According to our tri-captain Joe Williams, orders from Eaton were not to wear the armbands on the field Saturday. We went over Friday with hopes of receiving some answers to questions we felt were important to us as members of the football team and students at The University of Wyoming. What's wrong with a question?

Phil White Jr., Editor-In-Chief of the student newspaper the Branding Iron, knew the ramifications of what seems like a simple inquiry, "What's wrong with a question?" He details decades of civil rights abuses and racism in Wyoming in his recently published book, *Wyoming in Mid-Century: Prejudice, Protest and the "Black 14."*

According to a Branding Iron article of October 23, 1969, White resigned shortly after our dismissal in 1969, saying he was bowing to the wishes of most U.W. students who apparently do not want to read anything about racism or the Vietnam War or the urban crisis or drugs or prison abuses or politics. "After all," White said, "we don't have any problems here in Wyoming and we don't want any."

Before the game, demonstrations were in full force outside and in the parking lots leading to War Memorial stadium that Saturday. The fans overwhelmingly showed who they favored by wearing armbands of their own…"We support Coach Lloyd Eaton." The Black Students Alliance had its share of supporters as well, with protestors including professors and the Black 14 marching and carrying signs that left no doubt about the messages "What If God Is Black, Does Wyoming have a conscience?,

If we can't be men, we can't be Cowboys, Governor Who?, Have you thought about your constitution?, Is God racist?, First a man, then an athlete, We 14 may lose a lot, but we do it for the Blacks who follow."

The news media were tripping over themselves trying to get reactions! All three national networks were represented, as well as local Wyoming stations and those from Denver. It was hard to move or march in this case. Sports Illustrated ran a three page article that carried the headline "No Defeats, Loads Of Trouble." It also included a picture with 10 of the Black 14 sitting on the steps of the Wyoming Union. We did not look happy and for good reason. Jet Magazine featured a front cover headline, "Inside story of Fired Black Athletes." Reporters didn't appear to care much about who they were getting quotes from, never really knowing if what was said was true or not. But if it had to do with the Black 14 versus the Mormons? That was all they needed. Never bothering to check with us individually. I guess that would have taken too much effort. They had what they needed and they ran with it.

Letters to the Editor of the Casper Star-Tribune:

"The Cowboy Slave Traders appear to have prevailed, headed by Massa Eaton and backed by those other great humanitarians...the Grand Old Grads (who know a win-loss record when they see one, even if they don't know anything else)."

A former state representative wrote..."May I remind you readers that one of our free agencies, given by the Constitution, is Freedom of Religion." "May I remind you readers that it was your tax dollar that was giving most of these Negroes a free scholarship to gain an education and play football in Wyoming. You and I are paying for this and then they have the unmitigated gall to pull something like this." The letter said.

That attitude carried throughout the state. The Casper Quarterback Club, the Rock Springs City Council, and the University of Wyoming Alumni Association supported the coach without any of them contacting us.

However, the UW Student Senate adopted a resolution by a 15-3 vote, alleging that "Coach Eaton refused to grant a rational forum for discussion, choosing instead to degrade and arbitrarily dismiss each player...." The resolution went on to say the ASUW Senate "expresses its shock at the callous insensitive treatment afforded 14 Black athletes....The actions of Coach Eaton and the board of trustees were not only uncompromising, but unjust and totally wrong."

Meanwhile, The Denver Post editorialized that..."For a coach at the University of Wyoming or elsewhere to issue an edict that football players...may not protest policies they think are racist at Brigham Young University is an outrage. It is to suggest that football players are less than human and that they can be deprived of rights which the Constitution of the United States guarantees to other American citizens."

By this time some of us started receiving threatening phone calls and since gun racks were prominent fixtures in trucks driven by so many fans...these warnings were taken seriously! I was armed for the remainder of my time at the University of Wyoming.

As for the game which included a confederate flag being hoisted and visible until the fourth quarter, all-White Wyoming defeated all-White BYU 40-7. After the contest Eaton said, "The victory was the most satisfying one I've ever had in coaching."

RULE? WHAT RULE?

Four days after our dismissal, President Carlson and Coach Eaton held a news conference on campus to announce that the coach's rule, prohibiting student athletes from participating in demonstrations, was being amended to apply only while on the playing field. However, Eaton said the rule under which we were dismissed from the team remained in effect this year and we would not be reinstated for the remainder of this season. But at the end of the year, "Each can come in individually and review his situation," he said.

Following this four Black track members…Huey Johnson, Grady Manning, Mike Frazier and Jerry Miller quit the team in protest of our dismissals. Two were Western Athletic Conference champions in their individual events.

President Carlson was quoted as saying, "We've all made errors in this thing." But by errors he meant procedural activities, such as not immediately making information available to news media. President Carlson was also reported as saying, "The players themselves stated they would not play for Coach Lloyd Eaton."

Carlson continued, "The coaching staff had expressed during discussions, the day of the dismissals, a willingness to reinstate the players if they would participate in the Saturday game against BYU without armbands." But he then said,"the players would not accept this."

I was at a loss for words then, as a 19 year old…and I'm still speechless after reading that again, five decades later! People who are supposed to be held in such high esteem have turned out to be blatant liars. How do they live with themselves? I know I may be sounding a little naive…maybe it's because I am. But I know God exists, of that I'm sure. While some might think they may be getting away with something now, God can…and will make things right! His time is not our time. I wanted immediacy in dealing with this situation: but just because it didn't happen when I wanted it to…age and experiences have shown me He hasn't forgotten the injustice.

Still, I couldn't help but think about how hard I worked to achieve my dreams…only to have this nightmare come to life.

CHAPTER 2

A Child - Then a Man, With Little In Between

◆ ◆ ◆

MID 1950'S...ALSUMA, OKLAHOMA. ABOUT EIGHT miles southeast of Tulsa. It's a segregated, basically poor community with a lot of pride and some of the best honky tonks in the area. It's where my grandmother lives with her mother, on a little plot of land they call home and the family loves to visit. We called it, affectionately, the country. A lot of love for a place that doesn't even have running water. That also means the toilet is outside, which is where you find a couple of clever kids---or so they think.

We weren't exactly collecting money like millionaires! However, the stench from inside the outhouse couldn't drive a couple of broke boys from their treasure. Nickels, dimes, dollars.....for the taking. Our mistake was flashing the recovered loot, after a thorough cleaning, of course.

My great grandma was careful after that. If she went to the outhouse, her money went under her mattress. If not...there was always the handy, but smelly slop jar to do her business in the comfort of her bedroom; no worries about her dwindling retirement. We rebounded as youngsters can. In this case, because our days were filled with long lasting treasures...of the mind. Little money, but plenty of memories!

Growing up in the rural southwest meant hot humid summer weather, crawdad fishing and dirt roads, minus street lights. That takes some getting used to, but few did. However, sometimes, when you're fortunate ...you can still arrive at your destination, even when you don't exactly know where you're going.

I never worried about it ---I knew Carl, my older cousin, had that covered...always does. Sometimes we might pay a visit to one of the neighbor's yards. There, the next round of "anybody badder than me?" was usually in full swing and being judged, blow by blow. Shame on the loser, who would rather pull something out of the outhouse toilet, than face the taunts and looks of the audience or other competitors.

Carl could lay it on thicker than most. He wanted and demanded respect and felt he couldn't get it if his little cousin got his butt kicked from one end of the yard...to the other. Carl's mean spirit wasn't always obvious though. He would pick his spots. Like the time he relieved himself in a fresh supply of well-water. Good thing someone saw him!

As he grew older, the bolder Carl become. Jail, then prison served as his temporary address and eventually his permanent one for a while. A couple of 10 to 25 year terms solidified that fact. Some felt Carl was dealt a bad hand. His mother was in a mental institution, and his father died while Carl was young. So his actions, while not condoned, were not shocking to some in the family. He was perceived as a misguided kid. Carl used that kind of sympathy for all it was worth.

Long before things went all the way downhill for Carl, my young mother and I left Tulsa and traveled 176 miles north and settled in Wichita, Kansas.

Mama would be the first to admit that her little man was an accident...and a near death warrant for both. When she brought me into the world in 1950, she was only 15 1/2 years old. Her mother could have killed her. Actually, her life, as she knew it was over, but she saved her son's. Which meant going against the best meaning family members' idea to get rid of me. No place for this scenario in the conservative 50's still decades before the "babies making babies" situation we live with today.

But she was determined to make it and the same for me. I would know the mistakes she made and how to avoid the pitfalls she had encountered. I will make something of myself and not be stuck with an eighth grade education like her. She takes to the task of "schooling" me with the kind of focus that surely would produce her desired results. Another major failure is not an option for either of us.

Her job as a waitress prevented my mother from being home when I arrived from my half-day of school. No problem: I would learn, not only the best route from school, but also how to navigate the kitchen. Lunch soon became a source of pride for me, soup and sandwiches my forte. What was the big deal? Can of soup…add water, stir…fire it up! Mama's praise and encouragement inflated my little chest to man-sized dimensions.

But learning my ABC's produced the opposite effect. Mama, in her dogged determination to make her son a success, couldn't understand why I was having such a hard time! She didn't know her teaching methods would make a drill sergeant flinch. If I couldn't remember what followed "r"- I didn't have to guess what came next, even if I couldn't spell strap.

This reward and punishment approach made me an early candidate for a mental ward. I was scared sick, because Mama didn't know her own strength once she started on the down stroke with that strap. I could swear sparks flew from that thing and a few sympathetic neighbors would agree!

Bed time offered little comfort, not with the possibility of my welts being bathed in urine. This was the case more often than not. No matter how many times I would go to the bathroom before bed, too often I would wake up on saturated sheets and with the smell of ammonia punching out my nostrils. I knew my nose was just the starting point…soon, Mama and that strap would be working on my little wet ass.

In her defense, she was trying to change me the only way she knew how. There were no doctors on Oprah telling her how to raise her child. In fact there was no Oprah. Even if there was, when would she have time to watch and learn, while trying to keep us from being kicked out into the street? My dad was back in Oklahoma raising his "own" family. No time for this extra little crumb snatcher...in fact, there was still the question, in his mind, of whether or not I was his kid.

It's the way it was, trial and error, punishment and reward. I accepted it and Mama delivered it. But we would make it, as long as there was a God above and friends to help during the tough times. I just wished God and those friends were a little more visible and vocal, during the punishment part.

The situation would soon improve for Mama thanks to William. He was a single, hardworking employee for the city. "Hector the garbage collector" is what some called him; but Mama saw him as a companion, someone who would share more than her bed. Those newspaper coupons he brought home also came in handy. They were more than trash in that newly formed household!

I, even at my young age, quickly recognized the implications of all the changes. No longer was I "the man" of the house. The larger pieces of chicken now had William's name on them. There was also a change going on in my mama's bedroom--no more open door policy. That became graphically obvious one Halloween, when full of excitement I didn't knock. I'm sure my face instantly resembled the new grotesque mask I desperately wanted to show her.

Confusion, worry, and astonishment shot through me with the speed of a bullet. In its wake R.I.P. was the appropriate epithet for what used to be my innocence. But before that was truly realized, how about some answers? Was my mama being hurt? Captain Kangaroo, Bunny Rabbit, and Mister Green Jeans never prepared me for this!

Later, Mama tried to explain. I could tell she was uncomfortable and upset, a lot like she was last Thanksgiving. Considerable time had been spent on the holiday in school: drawing, talking and reading about it. The cornbread dressing, giblet gravy, sweet potato pies--candied yams! I was ready! But she wasn't...hardly, she was broke. But, with tears in her eyes she vowed we would have a good Thanksgiving and we did. She could be like that too! A provider, thanks to friends who helped her serve up the kind of love only a caring mother can.

However, this time I wasn't ready to accept what she tried to feed me....too much had changed. The bedroom scene was just the latest example. In my mind, I was no longer the focus of her love and attention, and of course I was right. Once you've been the only man in a woman's life, I learned quickly...it's hard to share, especially at five or six. I recognized that even then. I also felt something had to be done about the situation, and unknowingly set in motion events that would alter my life for years.

Growing up too Fast

Solving the situation seemed simple, one of us had to go. Either it was William, who appeared to have settled into a comfortable lifestyle or me. So I decided to hit the road...literally. I had a friend who lived near the freeway that could carry me back to my grandmother's house in Alsuma, Oklahoma. My observance during our trips from Oklahoma and Kansas and vice versa, assured me it was the correct route and after navigating my way home from kindergarten, I felt empowered with the ability to make a successful getaway.

During the weekend of my escape I told my mother I was spending the night with my friend. His mother, to the best of my memory, never inquired how my mother felt about this arrangement. I stayed with every intention of hitting the highway the next morning. Everything appeared to be progressing perfectly. I don't remember if I had any funds to pay for this trip. More than likely my idea was to hitchhike almost 200 miles.

I left my friend's house the next morning and had traveled about a block or so when a policeman, while I was heading to the freeway, pulled up alongside of me and showed me a picture and asked...is this you? Yup...guilty as charged officer. Then, fear I had never known came over me...leaving me with a feeling of dread, even though I couldn't comprehend its definition. I just know my stomach was in knots and the lump in my desert dry throat felt like it was the size of a watermelon. I was in big trouble, I knew that...and realizing my mama had a right hand that would rival Bob Gibson's, my butt had no chance of escape! Then, as if the clouds parted, my grandmother showed up out of nowhere! "Don't you touch a hair on that boy's head" she said! With that and as Mama smoldered...I snuggled a little closer to Grandma...and maybe even whimpered a bit.

Make no mistake....the situation that initiated my attempted "break" hadn't changed and my acting up, was far from over....unfortunately.

My search for new knowledge and mischief was helped by Brian. He, like Carl, was my cousin and senior by five years. No one was cooler than Brian. He had his own gang and didn't take anything from hardly anyone. He basically did what he wanted, even when it came to girls.

Darlene Cooper had to be THE finest thing I had ever seen. That kind of "tongue tied" fine--where, if you opened your mouth to speak, the only thing that came out was the last of your nerve. It was long gone.

I thought girls like that were to be admired and dreamed about. But Brian knew her inner needs and had no problem letting her know that he knew. "Come here...now!" That was the usual command he would give to Darlene. No need to take the long route, I guess.

When Brian delivered that order one day, it seemed to put Darlene into some kind of hypnotic trance, because she went to him like a zombie. Each step she took toward him...sliced into my heart.

Brian eventually "broke" it all down for his young cousin in book form...dirty books. The first time can be awkward for a grown up, to say nothing of a pre-teen. It wasn't perfect but by playing doctor with a young neighbor, the patient and I were making great progress. That is, until her mother came outside and chased me off with a shoe and some choice words...some, I had never heard.

Brian helped me to get over that with one of those "you have to get back on that horse" kind of speeches. Brian never seemed overly fazed by anything. He could charm the prettiest girl or talk you into places you have no business being. Like, the middle of a free-for-all gang fight, in which you're taking on someone almost a teenager!

Most of my days and nights were filled with that kind of fun. Trying to prove who could be the best thief, became another way to kill some time. The price tags were used to decide the champ. But the size of the prizes were rarely much larger than a bag of cookies or potato chips. I knew I really wasn't cut out for this when, on one occasion, an owner ran out of her store shouting "bring me back my pies!" Guess who turned around and handed the lady her pie? I never lived that one down, but I felt better.

These outings had become the replacement for my mother's attention, her time...and her love. I didn't know it then of course. Who had that kind of insight at my age? I was barely eight. It was always on to the next day, and the experiences that developed along the way. There were no thoughts about the future really and my mama was seemingly occupied, with no time for me. Besides, considering the climate around the globe, there wasn't much to look forward to. The Russians were going to blow everyone in America into the ground and there was nothing a fall-out shelter could do, despite the hopes of people who could afford one.

If you were me and my friends, your only hope were those silly drills you were taught in school. Cover and duck your head!! Years later I would wonder why they didn't teach me to kiss my butt good-bye as well.

BACK TO T-TOWN

Tulsa the second time around offered eye-opening revelations. I realized for the first time in my young life the color of my skin carried more of an impact than I had ever thought about or could have imagined.

My discovery was an accident, and carried the impact of a hammer slamming into my thumb.

The revelation came during one of my first paying jobs. Any money was appreciated and thanks to an uncle, I would have more than marbles to shake in my pockets. Talk about your ego booster! Not only because of the jingle in my pants, but it also helped to restore my belief that I was a man---just smaller than most. Lunch meant a trip to one of the few restaurants in Claremore, Oklahoma. There I took a table with other men. Nothing stood out about this until I looked to my left. It provided me with a straight line of sight through the kitchen and into the dining room. Apparently no one else wanted the seat because of the view.

The table cloths were white and so were the faces of the other customers. Why hadn't this stood out before? Why hadn't I noticed? But once this observation started to sink in, it did so with the speed of a super computer.

The meals looked the same, as far as I could tell. But the people who ate with me looked like me---same color. A different shade than those on the other side of the building. The surroundings were different too. There were no table cloths on my side of the kitchen. The lighting was poor and the walls didn't have pictures, just a lot of wood. No one else seemed to notice. Although I couldn't get an immediate explanation, I locked the experience away in my little brain. Something else for me to review at a later time when I could bend my uncle's ear without an audience.

I never got around to it. But the difference I saw and experienced that day became more apparent a few months later when I enrolled in my first integrated school. I felt the usual uneasiness that comes with being one of the new guys in class, but this was different. I had gone from looking like everyone else, to someone who stood out because of my color. I had become a minority, even though I didn't really know what that meant.

Credit here has to go to my mom, who always taught me I wasn't better than anyone else and no one was any better than I was. Another one of those defining periods in my life---but again, I wouldn't really appreciate it for a few years.

By the next semester I moved and changed schools. No integration, but a lot of problems. Being the new kid in class carried the same uneasy feelings, however my skin color wasn't the issue, the bullies were. They wanted to take my money and my pride. I had to fight daily to keep both. I had no big brothers who could help me out in these scrapes. It was me against whomever and whatever the day served up.

Another move and a change in schools helped considerably. A fresh start meant new subjects and classmates. I enjoyed the calmer environment. But I wasn't motivated by the books. Grades didn't hold the same importance of a good softball game or checking out the latest 45 on a turn table. Life was good just the way it was: average grades, good enough to keep my mom off my back and music that made me want to move!

My relationship with Mama was beginning to settle into more of a younger brother-older sister situation...rather than mom and son. William left when the relocation back to Tulsa was made. But before that, I accepted William and his role in the family. Mama took classes, got her G.E.D., and continued her studies aimed at something that would, if she decided, elevate her beyond domestic work.

This was never something she talked about. In fact, she put as much into cleaning someone else's house as she did her own. She liked the families she worked for and if she didn't---she would let them know it. She could drop to her hands and knees to clean dirty floors, but walk out of a house with all her pride still intact. Head up, shoulders and back straight, like she owned the world...or a large piece of it! She passed that on to me and had me continuously working at an early age. I would soon purchase my own clothes and give Mama her share of my money, while still taking care of my chores (didn't everyone?).

She was slowly molding me into the kind of man a woman would love to have. I didn't have a clue, but knew what was expected---and what wouldn't be tolerated.

Surprise! Now Try This

I was young, but felt much older. For example, despite being a pre-teen, I was smart enough to know I didn't want to take the paths of my two older cousins. Brian and Carl would both end up in jail and eventually the penitentiary. That helped to distance me and forced me to change my ways of thinking.

Secretly, I hoped it would lead to an easier life while trying to make it from one day to the next. The idea of having cops banging on my door at some ridiculous hour, had no appeal. Neither did the prospect of feeling scared nearly every waking moment. Plus, I liked freedom, even though I didn't really know what the alternative felt like.

If I was going to continue enjoying it, another change was in order. That would happen sooner than I expected, just not the way I envisioned. It literally materialized while Mama was doing my wash. She found a little something extra in the front of my underwear. How could this be, I thought? Not even in junior high school...and capable of making babies!

Gone forever were the days of care-free sex! I was too young to be having it in the first place, but old enough to realize, during the next encounter...protection would have to be in place. Talk about being bummed. Even worse was Mama's lesson on how to help relieve my desires. I couldn't spell masturbation, but knew enough about it to know "shooting off"...the terminology my mother used, wasn't exactly the correct slang that described what I was supposed to do.

Life's lessons and the way they affect us! They are the things that could fill a book! You think? The discovery of sex, first involving my mother and now me...was certainly not something I could have expected in the first few years of my existence. Throw in my introduction to crime and integration and it's an understatement to say I was moving fast, but to what?

Four decades later, I would still be searching for an answer. In my most mature mind I realized that making sense out of a senseless world is not something easily achieved...if ever. While that should have been obvious, how many things are? Especially when you haven't lived long enough to grow facial hair? The complexities of a world full of contradictions can take their toll on us all. But the individual experiences can serve as conductors---with knowledge the insulation, sometimes!

IN SEARCH OF SOMETHING

Maybe it was the frustration with my life and the gnawing need to do more with it; or it was the repetitive message from others to think hard about my future, but I was beginning to realize my perspective was changing...I just don't know exactly when it started. What I did know was that I was tired of the same old, same old about my life; aimlessly wandering through my days, thinking mostly about what my next paycheck would get me.

I started buying the majority of my clothes when I entered seventh grade, thanks in large part to Mama's insistence. And seeing how it was her idea for me to get a job, she expected and received half of my money. I didn't really mind pitching in. William was history and I was again the man. With that distinction came certain obligations. Besides, I wanted to help ease her burden. She worked hard for her money, but there never seemed to be enough to go around. That was painfully evident the time I tried to help her with her budget. Mama, in tears, thought she had lost or was shorted $20. As it turned out, it was money she had already spent. It hurt me. Although an only child, I was thankful there were no more mouths to feed or bodies to clothe.

This is probably one of the reasons I started seriously thinking about my own future. Because of my two cousins' career of crime, I knew I didn't want money to be a problem when I became a real man. So interest in my studies picked up and the honor roll became a goal. I would begin to achieve it with regularity. Student government was my next target. I lost my first run for an office, but that would be my last defeat. Within two years I would ascend to the presidency of my junior high school student council!

One of the biggest steps I took led me to the football field. Again, it was a message from someone who cared that started me on my way. "Your mama will never be able to put you through college. You'd better start thinking about athletics as a way to help you get there!" It made sense to me to add sports to my improving studies and double my chances of getting to college. Which also got me to thinking more about my turn-around. So far, so good, why not stay the course? I couldn't deny that things were a lot better. Now I began each day with a positive purpose directed at a goal. I was now hearing everything, that for so long, was in-one-ear and out-the-other. Plus, I began to chart my success from the wisdom I picked up from others. I couldn't shake the obvious, it was working!

I had rarely tried to play football, but certainly thought I was big enough, having gained most of my height by the time I was in the sixth grade. When I hit the gridiron in the seventh, I was 5'10". Not exactly Wilt Chamberlain, but taller than most my age and with enough weight that no one was calling me "Stilt."

George Washington Carver Jr. High School is located off Greenwood Street, which then was the heart of North Tulsa. Early in the 20th century it was the prominent section of what was once known as America's "Black Wall Street" because of all the successful African-American businesses that lined it. It was "hopping," as we used to say. That is until one of the most devastating massacres in U.S. history destroyed it in 1921. A White mob attacked residents, homes, and looted businesses. Credible estimates put the number killed between 50 and 300, with countless injuries, and 10,000 Blacks left homeless. It is believed an encounter between an African American man and a White female fueled the "riot," with racially charged newspaper editorials literally fanning the flames.

By 1962, while not nearly what it used to be, Greenwood was vibrant and helped to form a popular three letter name for a singing group, the GAP band, which stands for Greenwood, Archer and Pine Streets.

Carver Jr. High School is also a cornerstone and served as my first introduction to football. I didn't know a whole lot about the sport or the equipment. Let's start with the shoes or "spikes," as we called them. Black high-tops…worn by basically everybody and not just the linemen. They were hand-me-downs…that had been handed down. No Nikes' for sure.

The practice jerseys were oversized donations from the high school, along with the pads. But you couldn't find a prouder player when I earned my first uniform. I had made the Carver Cats team… with very little knowledge of how to play this game! Considering that, I was quickly placed at the center position. Just count, snap the ball… and go get in the way of that guy over there. The following year I reversed that from the snap-er, to the snap-ee---by switching to quarterback. I also was playing more defensive back and getting pretty good at it! My final year at Carver, we could compete with anyone, but lost the city championship eight-nothing, in one of the coldest games I had the misfortune of playing. I never left the field…and with no gloves, my hands were slicker than ice. I can't count the number of fumbles. A very disappointing experience.

Hallowed Ground

> "Dear Booker T. Washington High School, the pride of the great Southwest. You're a symbol of light for many a youth, by pointing the way to life's best."
>
> C.B. Neely- BTWHS Vocal Musical Instructor 1918-1960

Booker T. Washington High School had me in its grasp long before I left Carver. Not that there were that many choices, thanks to segregation.

But that was about to become history. Regardless, this was going to be my home even when I barely had a real one to lay my head in. To those on the outside, it's hard to describe the attraction: before all the championships, noted alumni, and academic achievements, BTW was it for me. If I had to choose a word to describe why…"Pride" would be at the top of my list.

From day one you were instilled with it. In everything you did, you did it with pride. You might not have the best clothes…but if you were smart, you made sure they were washed and pressed…and your hair was "right" before you arrived at school. You held your head high and ready to compete…in everything! In the classroom, on the athletic fields, in chorus, in band, as a majorette, a cheerleader, in plays, in the numerous organizations, and in "Hi Jinks"…the all-school talent show. You better show up ready …or be embarrassed.

It was imprinted in you by the caring and engaged teachers, the boisterous and tough coaches…even your unforgiving fellow students, when you didn't do something the right way. Which happened a lot to first year arrivals, who were given the embarrassing title of "Sloppy Sophomores." "Jiving Juniors" and most assuredly, "Sophisticated Seniors" knew better. For example, not to go up the down staircase. It happened to me and it was in sight of a sharp-eyed senior. She made sure everyone, within the sound of her voice, knew the "crime" I had committed. No place to run…no place to hide. You just take it and learn quickly!

This generally started the very first day you walked through the doors of BTW and were greeted by that orange and black Hornet. You could tell it meant business, a hint…you would be advised to take!

This attitude carried over to athletics, even though this was not an area that had yielded a lot of success. There were individuals who stood out and made it to the pros, but collectively those state championships had not materialized since integration. During segregation it was just the opposite, where under the late legendary football coach, Seymour Williams, the Hornets won 17 Oklahoma Interscholastic Negro Association State Titles from 1921 to 1955.

That wasn't lost on us in 1967. Practices started out as they usually did…very intense. But maybe because it was the last opportunity for seniors like myself, there was an urgency and a focus. There was also a bitter taste that lingered from junior high school. A feeling that many injustices had come our way when we played. It went beyond bad or questionable calls. There were players who would be pronounced ineligible, because of residency, just days away from a championship game. Whether perceived or true, why would these things happen now? We felt the fact that we were an all-Black team had something to do with what was happening. So this year we were committed to changing our situation. Guess you could say we had a severe case of the "for reals." We would not be denied or deterred. Not this year!

The plan was simple…the officials couldn't call back all the touchdowns. Potentially, on every play there is an opportunity for a flag to fly. A flinch of a hand or foot. Too much emphasis after a tackle, a wayward elbow, someone is inches off or over the line of scrimmage, illegal formation, you name it! Then you get upset and things usually go from bad to worse! Your reaction or objection to the call could send you out of the game…or you could be suspended, for who knows how long? We had learned from previous scenarios, and this year…it was going to be different for BTW. Soon the whole state would know!

Our goal was to score 12 touchdowns a game (figuring, if half of those were called back, we still had at least 36 points) and pitch a shutout on defense. We fell a little short in the first game, but still eased past East Central, 33 to 6. Webster would fall next, 56 to 0. Muskogee Manual, a rival, would taste defeat, 34 to 0. Bartlesville Sooner, 53 to 0. McClain, 49 to 0. McAlester, 28 to 0.

Oklahoma City Douglass (arguably the most anticipated game of the year), 31 to 0. Memorial and their talented tailback Kent Bays, 26 to 0. (Kent powered the Chargers over the Hornets the year before, by gaining over 170 yards rushing. He and I would renew acquaintances as freshmen in college).

We had shut out seven straight opponents! Who does that? There was one game left in the regular season, and we wanted desperately to add one more goose egg to our record. Sadly it didn't happen. The zebras "gave" a touchdown to Sapulpa and its bruising 240 pound running back. That's my story and I'm sticking to it. We won the game 26 to 6.

We were in uncharted territory, a real first, as the state playoffs loomed large! How would we react? Were we really capable of going all the way? A lot of naysayers felt we had done all we could do. We were about to see what this football crazy state really has to offer, especially since we were playing in the biggest class of high schools. But surprise! It was more of the same in the semi-finals as we blanked Ponca City 35 to 0!

One more mountain to climb and it might as well have been Kilimanjaro according to "people in the know." No Black school had EVER achieved a state football title! Our feeling? 'Bout time for that to change!

There was no fear, but plenty of anticipation. It showed during spirited practices, not only among the players, but the coaching staff as well. They wanted to surprise the top ranked and undefeated Midwest City Bombers, by changing almost everything we did! We revised our defensive assignments and became super conservative on offense. As players, we were frustrated. Why fix it, if it's not broken? Or put it this way, why don't we see if they can stop us before going to plan B? So we rolled into Oklahoma City, in the biggest game of our lives, with questions among ourselves, especially on defense.

My new assignment had me covering, on certain alignments, over half the field from my safety position. The idea was to provide extra help to the cornerbacks. Well, early in the game it became abundantly clear this was not going to work, as one of the Bombers' receivers got loose down the sideline and headed for a touchdown. I gave him a good bump, to knock him off stride and out of bounds. But I didn't get all of him and he "walked the chalk" as we used to say…all the way into the end zone.

Talk about getting our attention! They definitely had it now. Initially, we didn't sweat it or get too down…and there was no finger pointing, not even when Midwest City scored again, on pretty much the same play! This time I gave it all I had…he kept his balance and scored. We hadn't given up this many points throughout the entire season! Just 12 in 10 games! Now we headed into half-time down 14 to 3. More uncharted territory, this time filled with questions.

TIME FOR A CHANGE

There was no shouting during intermission…but we convinced our defensive coach to go back to what brought us here. However offensively, the head coach planned on staying the conservative course, hoping not to make any mistakes, I guess. We had speed to burn, on the field and on the bench. We had a quarterback who could effectively pass or run. We had major college receivers in the making. WE AVERAGE 37 POINTS A GAME!! Why, oh why, were we playing conservative? Frustration was starting to mount as we jogged back onto the field.

We stopped their scoring and approached the fourth quarter still down 14-3. Midwest City was starting to feel pretty good about itself and headed into the fourth quarter proudly displaying four fingers to signify only one quarter to go. Then things began to change…did they ever.

Our quarterback, Floyd "Bo" Tiger, was probably the most frustrated person in the sold-out stadium. But there were plenty of fans who let us know what they were thinking. They were loud and very clear. The comments were on the brink of getting real ugly. One of our backup centers, Alvin Mayberry, entered the game and gave Bo another conservative call from the bench. Basically, it was the same I-formation, off tackle play, that had been averaging about five yards a carry. But Oliver Ziegler, our 175 pound tailback, was unbelievably dangerous in the open field. Tonight he wasn't given the chance to show it, making those five yard gains tougher than they needed to be. Plus, we had pass plays off that formation and a sweet counter as well.

Bo turned to John Winesberry, a sophomore wide receiver, and defiantly changed the play. You have to understand, it took some "huge ones" for Bo to do that, and were we glad he had 'em. He faked the run to Zeigler, and found a wide open Winesberry for one of the biggest touchdowns of his career, and he would have a bunch. The stadium exploded and the fans charged out of the stands, shouting their approval.

On the ensuing kickoff we forced a fumble on their fifteen...and Bo took it in from the three yard line. 17-14 Hornets! Very next possession, Bo waved off another conservative call from the bench and found Winesberry for a 21 yard touchdown. We scored 27 points in the fourth quarter! Everyone not wearing orange and black had a stunned look of disbelief.

We were state champs, 30 to 14! The celebration could probably be heard all the way back to Tulsa, where a high school championship had not been celebrated since 1946!

The City of Tulsa raised money and sent the entire team to Miami, Florida and the Orange Bowl...where The University of Oklahoma held off Tennessee 26-24. In the middle of the Sooner's defensive lineup was All-America and legendary Hornet, Granville Liggins. You think they love their high school football in Oklahoma?

Winesberry and Reuben Gant were part of a talented group of sophomores who would celebrate three straight state titles by the Hornets. Winesberry starred for Stanford and led that team to a 13-12 upset over Michigan in the 1972 Rose Bowl. Winesberry, who passed away in 2005, had 112 yards in receptions during that game. His playing career was cut short by injuries. Gant, a big target at receiver, went on to Oklahoma State, where he would become an NFL first round draft pick of Buffalo. He played seven seasons with the Bills.

The Hornets followed those three consecutive titles by adding two more over the next four years. At this printing, Booker T. has nine state championships in football.

The championship was icing for my senior year, which also included a president of Student Council post and the honor of being named Mr. Hornet. Because of God's grace, my dreams are coming true...my plan is working. But, where would I go from here? Would this be as good as it gets for me? What would I tell my 17-year-old self today? How about something like this: "Well son, I've got some good news and some bad. Oh yeah, better go out and pick up some warm underwear, 'cause you're gonna need it!"

CHAPTER 3

"...How They Run—Yes Run—When They Hear Him Come..."

THE FLIGHT TO DENVER WAS my first ride on an airplane and it was smooth. So I'm thinking this isn't half bad, but when we left Stapleton International Airport headed for Laramie, that all changed. I thought surely I was going to die as we bounced and shimmed, up and down, for the entire flight! Thankfully only 131 miles separate the two cities, but when the pilot announced we were about to land, I honestly wanted to know---where? Nothing but mountains out my window. Welcome to Big Sky country!

My recruitment did not include a trip to Wyoming. The process was pretty simple really. My high school head coach tells me "Wyoming is interested in you. Sounds like a good opportunity. I think you should take it." That was it. The Wyoming coach/recruiter didn't even visit my home to meet my mother. They wanted me, but in my mind, I wasn't a high priority. I wasn't a thousand yard rusher, who scored 25 touchdowns. I may have won a state championship, but I was a defensive back, a position that didn't receive respect until the last couple of decades.

When I competed, offensive players in the skilled positions (quarterbacks, running backs, and receivers), were sent to the defensive backfield side of the ball if they couldn't make it offensively. Which made no sense. Defensive backs have to master the art of running backwards, turning and running with fast, usually tall, big receivers or have the ability to break off that coverage, head back toward the line of scrimmage and tackle a 225 pound ball carrier, who is probably escorted by a couple of sizeable offensive linemen---and oh yeah, that ball carrier could turn into a receiver, so be sure that's covered too. It's unfair to tell an offensive player to try and become a defensive back without a lot of practice. Defensive backs are the last line of defense. If they fail, the opponents' mascot is doing its thing and the scoreboard is going off like it's the fourth of July.

I was particularly fond of the safety position. You get to do all those fun things that are part of a defensive back's job...plus you patrol the field like a centerfielder in baseball. I believed when the ball leaves the quarterback's hand, it becomes anybody's ball. I lived for the interception, even more than the big hit that would have everybody oohing and awing. I'm thinking touchdown baby, Pick 6!

My first practice with the freshman team (freshmen were not allowed to play varsity football until 1972) I counted 13 safeties. Wow! Nothing like a little competition I guess. I learned pretty quickly that the coaches used an overabundance of players to help sort out who would still be standing after the practices, freshmen games, spring practice, and two-a-days in the summer. I was told by some upperclassmen that only 10 or 11 of us were likely to advance to the varsity. There were more than 70 freshman players getting some kind of scholarship help and probably 35 others hoping to get a scholarship in 1968! Well over 100 players (This is little old Wyoming). What were Notre Dame, Oklahoma, and Michigan doing?

The quickest way to send players packing was the running of 40-yard sprints - over and over again. Remember, the altitude is 7200 feet above sea level, 2000 feet higher than mile high Denver, and oxygen is not allowed! If someone passes out, the coaches would just move the ball over...and keep going. By the way, you're being timed. Let's say you gave it your all the first sprint (and you can be sure you weren't the only one trying to impress). Now, the coaches know what to expect out of you, always. Whether you were…or thought you were…an All-America, the best in your town, city or state…it didn't matter. The practice field was a no coddling zone. That first night you could hear the suitcases thumping the floor, as former stars headed for the door…and home.

We played a four-game freshman schedule (Colorado twice, Air Force, and Colorado State). We won all the games…and by the first one, I had made captain. During one of those contests against Colorado, I received a pretty good lick on my right knee, when a teammate failed to inform me that I was about to be hit. It's called a "crack back block," one in which an opposing player hits a defender below the waist. Often your knee is the target. This usually happens while you are distracted or engaged with another opposing player; which is why you depend on your teammate to alert you to what is about to happen. It's now against the rules. I thought I was headed to the operating table. It hurt that bad!

As I hobbled toward the bench, I heard the Freshman Head Coach, Jack Taylor say…"Hey, where do you think you're going? Stay out there! What is this I hear about Black Power? Stay out there!" I was shocked, flabbergasted, and confused. I also was hurting. If this was his way to motivate and encourage me, he failed miserably! It was obvious he wasn't going to replace me, so for the first and only time, I allowed an opposing team to score. Their players could see I was hurt, so they came right at me, off tackle. I did what is called an "Ole!" Like a matador, I waved my invisible cape and gave the runner easy access to our end zone. Unbelievable!

We had what was called study hall, but you didn't study for your classes. You studied football! Often it was 10:00 p.m. or later when you were allowed to go back to your room…that's when you hit the books. Practice started around 2:30 in the afternoon, so it made for a long day. You did have dinner during this stretch. You were released, with just enough time to get to the cafeteria before it closed. We didn't have an athletic dormitory catering to jocks. Eat all you want, but you can't take it with you. After running for hours, food was not what I wanted...give me something to drink! I gained one pound my freshman year. That had to be by design. 'Ya think?

So, it was football and more football, with an ample amount of studying. I carried a full load, 15 hours. I was busy. Sadly, when there was time to relax and have fun...there were very few opportunities to socialize with girls. Again, I didn't take a recruiting trip to Laramie. I thought, with Denver only a couple of hours away and other universities even closer, there would be some coeds on campus. There were, just not that many Black ones. Because of that, they were like kids in a candy store. Similar to the football team, it was a numbers game and Black females were winning...big time. There were less than 10 of them on campus so they were outnumbered three or four to one. Dating White coeds was definitely frowned upon by the coaching staff...an unwritten rule. I would learn there were a few of those stipulations at Wyoming. One in particular will play a major role in my life, which we will discuss later. But right now, I'm miserable and very frustrated!

When the season ended, I had time to really look at my situation. Because without football, what was there for me in Laramie, Wyoming? I couldn't even take up skiing without risking my scholarship because of potential injuries. The situation became too much for me to handle, so with tears in my eyes I headed over to the athletic offices and told a coach my intention of going back to Tulsa. I told him there was no social life here for me and I'm going crazy. I was done, color me gone, aloha!

The coach came up with a proposal I couldn't believe. He asked me if I had a girlfriend. I said I did. (But we had broken up before I left for Laramie.) He asked if she was in college. Yup, I replied and began to wonder where he was going with this? He asked if she had at least a C average. Yes I said. Then he blew me away when he said, if she was willing, she could be here by January, for the second semester.

I dropped back into my seat in a daze and wondered if I heard him right! It would be a win-win for me, for my girl, and for the team... on two fronts. I would remain in Laramie and stay in "my lane" by not dating White coeds. Apparently the coaching staff realized this was a growing problem and I guess I was one of the first to benefit from this previously unknown solution.

To the best of my understanding, money in the general university fund enabled a move like this. It would also be applied to recruit other African-American females, some of whom didn't like the idea. I heard they thought they...and others who might follow, would be used to appease the growing number of Black athletes. Whatever the case, it worked for me and I was thankful to take advantage of this opportunity!

Now my concentration turned back to football, and spring football in particular. During these couple of months, I learned for the first time that my scholarship was not for four years. Well, it was...and it wasn't. Every year in spring ball you earned another year of your scholarship. So it gave the team an opportunity to reduce what you were receiving, make you so miserable that you quit, or they cut you altogether.

The conversation with the head coach would take place before you headed home for the summer---after you completed practices and a couple of spring games. It could go something like this "You want to play Cowboy football? Yeah coach! No, the coach might say, do you REALLY want to play Cowboy football? You bet coach, absolutely! Good, we're going to have to take half your tuition, books, and board. See you this summer and maintain your workout schedule."

Nice, huh? Fortunately for me, I only heard about this from others...and did not experience it for myself. So, I took off for home, and would get married in June. Another new beginning? You bet, but it would be in ways I couldn't even imagine.

With This Ring I'll Always Love You

My mother had beaten me to the punch. I didn't even know she was dating, so the fact she got married blew me away! Within weeks of my departure for Laramie, back in August, she started dating and became serious about Claude. He was a widower with three kids. Two boys and a girl. I was ten to fifteen years older, depending on the sibling. My mother was a pretty good cook (her peach cobbler, cornbread dressing, and fried chicken were outstanding!). But Claude? He is on a whole different level. He's one of those…use a pinch of this and a fist full of that… kind of cooks. And the combination of ingredients he uses will have you scratching your head, saying…I would have never thought of that!

He can "throw down" on anything, but his stuffed peppers, German chocolate cake, turkey and dressing, candied yams, stuffed pork chops, baked chicken, smoked barbecue brisket---are truly to die for! And homemade rolls? Please! That's how I first met him. Claude was a cook, barking out instructions at McCollum's restaurant on 11th Street, where I was a youngster washing dishes. Biggest pots and pans I had ever seen. Big enough for me to practically climb into! One of the enticements for the job (besides me needing the money) was getting a free meal…complete with one or two of Claude's rolls, yum! But I couldn't imagine that he would one day become my stepfather.

I mentioned that I gained only one pound during my first year at Wyoming. Well, with Claude doing the majority of our cooking, that changed, big time! Even though I was sticking to my workout routine supplied by the coaches, I picked up 30 pounds over the summer!! I went into a panic, knowing this was not good. Thankfully I had a park around the corner from our house. My workouts became super serious. Still, when I reported back to camp, the coaches were stunned.

When they last saw me I weighed 191 pounds. I was now 212. I was given orders to drop back below 200, or else they would have to make some changes in my position. They thought I had been goofing off all summer, which wasn't true. I blame it all on Claude. When we opened the season I was a svelte 203. Stretched out over my 6 foot, 2 inch frame I thought I looked slim. However, the coaches were not used to seeing defensive backs my size. When the year started, I was still a safety---and now a starter.

With that worked out, I wanted to tackle another problem.

WHAT IS A JERRY BERRY?

Jerry Berry? What is that? Who is that? My given name is Jerome Berry. But very shortly after my arrival in Laramie, I became Jerry Berry, at least that's what I was being called. I didn't make a lot of it at first, hoping it would stop. But oh no, it stuck! I didn't know in some cultures Jerome can become Jerry. This was new to me and I was not a fan. Early in my career, back in junior high school when I was running the football a lot, the announcers would say..."It's Berry on the carry." That had some appeal, I guess. But Jerry Berry? My first realization was that I would lose my identity. Nobody back in Tulsa knew who Jerry Berry was and certainly couldn't connect me with being a Hornet!

Inwardly, I was bummed. I tried to plead my case, especially to announcers, to no avail. In fact it seemed the more notoriety I received, the worse (in my opinion) it became.

THE 60'S – A DECADE OF DEATH AND DESTRUCTION

The issue with my new name was certainly nothing compared to what was happening all around me. Times were a-changing and had been for years. While segregation was basically a thing of the past...America was trapped in social, civil, and economic upheaval! During the 1960's the Vietnam War raged for years! It devastated our youth and turned the country against itself. Many who were fortunate to return from the war were never the same. They could sometimes be seen walking aimlessly down a street, dressed as if it was winter, when in reality the temperature was hovering around 100 degrees and the humidity was just as oppressive.

Demonstrations stretched from East to West...North to South, and all points in between. Many started or ended on college campuses. Every facet of our society was affected as opposition to the war grew. The peace movement was joined by civil rights organizations, women's liberation, Chicano protests, and factions of organized labor. Educators, clergy, journalists, and military veterans were also active participants.

During this 10-year stretch, President John F. Kennedy was assassinated, as were Medgar Evers, a NAACP field secretary, and Malcolm X. Add to that list Dr. Martin Luther King Junior and Former United States Attorney General, Robert Kennedy, who was seen by some to be destined to be the next President. In 1963 four girls, ages 11 to 14, were killed in Birmingham, Alabama, after some members of the Ku Klux Klan planted 16 sticks of dynamite beneath the steps of the 16th Street Baptist Church. At least 22 other parishioners were injured.

And America was burning! Harlem in '64, Watts in '65, Newark and Detroit in '67, and Chicago in '68, as racial and civil unrest spilled into the streets. They caused millions and millions of dollars in damage, untold deaths and injuries...and often total destruction of entire neighborhoods.

As an athlete...a college or pro athlete in particular, you are expected...in fact, demanded to, "Keep your eyes on the prize." Let nothing, a seemingly insurmountable deficit, injury, or human injustice deter you. KEEP YOUR EYES ON THE PRIZE! In reality---is that possible?

GAME TIME!

My introduction to real Cowboy football came my freshman season. Sure, we went undefeated during an abbreviated season (four games). But I'm talking big boy football...with big boy pads. Granted the Cowboys were coming off winning three straight Western Athletic Conference crowns, and this is when the WAC still included Arizona State, Arizona, and Utah. But on this Saturday, Wyoming was facing a Sun Devils team, which according to my count, would field at least 11 future NFL players: including two first-rounders, Linebacker Ron

Pritchard and wide receiver J.D Hill. Then throw in running back Art Malone, Larry Walton, and Fair Hooker.

No offense to our varsity, but I didn't think we had much of a chance. Arizona State was big, fast...and physical! But I didn't know Jack....or Jane.

Led on offense by Dave Hampton, soon to be an NFL star himself at running back, and Gene Huey, one of the last of the great two-way players (wide receiver and defensive back)...the Cowboys were more than up to the challenge of the 14th ranked Sun Devils. On defense, the team's strong suit, hard-hitting linebacker Jim House laid some heavy licks to bring ASU's offense to a crawl. Tackle Larry Nels, who would be drafted by the New York Giants, safety Dennis Devlin, soon the property of the Boston Patriots, and a young Tony McGee, a third-round selection of the Chicago Bears, helped take care of the rest.

Wyoming stunned not only Arizona State, but an 18-year-old freshman safety, who got a lesson that day on how Cowboy football is played. Left out of this picture is the man who orchestrated one of the most creative defensive attacks in all of college football...and eventually the National Football League. His name? Fritz Shurmur.

He was as fiery as his red hair, with a drill sergeant demeanor that demanded a player's attention. Attack his mode, failure his immense dislike. Shurmur was a man's man, from a defensive perspective...it was his calling card. Man for man defense...that made him my kind of man. He didn't play to lose, but to win. He was aggressive. A zone defense? Only if he had to. Because of this, opponents never knew from which direction Shurmur would attack. Rarely was the right side of his defense doing the same as the left side. Shurmur's stunts came from so many angles, they kept offensive coordinators and quarterbacks guessing. More often than not, a smart defensive back or linebacker benefited with an interception or fumble recovery.

From Wyandotte, Michigan, down the waterway from Detroit, Shurmur would offer his style of play to those willing to listen. From little Albion College, to the University of Wyoming. Then to the NFL with stops in Detroit, New England, the L.A. Rams, Arizona Cardinals, Green Bay (where as defensive coordinator, he guided the Packers to a Super Bowl win over New England in 1997) and Seattle. Liver cancer cut his life and career short in 1999 before he could coach the Seahawks. His nephew, Pat Shurmur, formerly head coach of the Cleveland Browns, was named head coach of the New York Giants in 2018.

One of my biggest regrets, when the subject is football, is that I wasn't able to play longer for Fritz. There were a couple of times during summer two-a-day practices, I wasn't sure if I would play at all! Tri-captain Joe Williams was burning me like toast. I wasn't used to that and was extremely embarrassed! Not once, but twice! It involved a drill in which, if a certain offensive alignment was recognized (more offensive backs, receivers, or possibly players on one side than we had), "trips" would be called, which meant I had to get over there...with the quickness! I didn't make it! Joe would catch a pass and be long gone. I was left to lick my wounds and gather up what was left of my pride. Consider it a lesson thoroughly learned. I certainly hoped so!

Cowboy Football

It's a beautiful day, gorgeous setting and a stadium full of anticipating fans. I am focused and sporting my usual game face. Stoic expression, all business baby. I don't think I belong...deep inside me, I know it. Now time to show it.

Split end Ron Hill, affectionately known as the Alabama buck, opens the scoring early in the second quarter on a 22-yard reception from Ed Synakowski. We will never trail, but that doesn't mean it was easy. Behind 13-nothing in the 3rd, Arizona is making a push, all the way to our 12-yard line.

A very familiar scenario is coming into focus. But this time, thanks to the "picture" Joe Williams gave me in practice, I am prepared for the Arizona runner sneaking out of his backfield. I intercept the pass at its apex and I'm hoping I don't get caught. Out of the corner of my eye I see our middle guard, Steve Adamson, waving at me to slow down! He wants to set up a convoy for me!

What? I want to try and show some speed here...and by all means score this touchdown! Instead of sticking to the sideline, I ease toward the middle of the field, looking over my shoulders for Arizona players. The escort is set and my teammates start taking them out, one by one! I go the distance...88 yards for the touchdown!! I'm exhausted, but thrilled. Wait! Is that a flag? Whew, it's on the Wildcats!

We win it 23 to 7. Not a bad start! Ten tackles, with eight unassisted, two for losses, and an 88-yard Pick 6. That brought on more than my share of regional, and even national exposure! Next?

When the term "Wild ,Wild West" is spoken or written, I often think of our next game against Air Force Academy, in Colorado Springs. It-was-crazy! The first two times they touched the ball offensively... they scored. Gary Baxter, their "obviously" talented quarterback, connected on 31 of 51 passes and threw for 388 yards. Flanker Ernie Jennings, who would be named a consensus All-America the following season, caught 15 of Baxter's throws for 131 yards. Not to be outdone, split end Mike Bolen had seven receptions, 155 yards...and the aforementioned two touchdowns!

"Stunned" couldn't begin to describe the way I felt, maybe "helpless" would be a better word. I would back pedal, turn, look over my shoulder and just watch as the receiver flew into the end zone. They weren't throwing the ball in my direction and there was simply not much I could do! I think only two passes were caught on me the entire game and they were for minimal yardage. The only thing we could hang our hat on, at this point, was their two missed extra point attempts. Still we trailed 15-3 midway through the second quarter.

Like a heavyweight boxer shaking off a left hook, we regained our composure and started to fight back! The offense put together a 15-play drive, which culminated with quarterback Gary Fox's one-yard score, on fourth down…with only 37 seconds left in the half. 15-10 Air Force at the break.

Time for some Cowboy football and all the pieces were coming together. Joe Williams, Frosty Franklin, and Tony Gibson were grinding out significant yards on the ground. Bob Jacobs was booming 60-yard punts and the defensive line was beginning to shine…with Larry Nels and Tony McGee starting to impose their will on the Falcons.

That may not sound correct when you consider their passing yards, but Nels would drop Baxter two consecutive times and McGee was in the midst of one of his best games…seven sacks! He also pulled off one of the most incredible plays I have had the joy of watching when he chased down a fast halfback on a reverse, before the runner could reach the line of scrimmage. Unbelievable! That runner didn't know our defensive end was one of the fastest players on the team, sporting a 4.4 time in the 40.

A 20-yard sprint by Joe Williams gave us our first lead…17-15 midway through the 3rd. The Falcons countered with a field goal. 18-17 Air Force, late in the quarter. The ensuing kickoff falls into the waiting arms of lineman Mel Hamilton, who advances to Wyoming's 44…basically mid-field. That set up another field goal for Jacobs. 20-18 Cowboys. The offense would add to it, by putting together an 11-play, 55-yard drive…highlighted by Franklin and Gibson runs and capped off by Paul Taylor's one-yard reception. Jacobs splits the uprights…27-18 Cowboys, 7:03 left.

But Air Force wasn't done…and right about now I'm thinking this must be the way it feels to play in the NFL – back and forth. You're up, you're down…and then you're up again. When is this thing going to end? Baxter navigates a nine play drive, and hits split end Charlie Longnecker for a nine-yard score. 27-25 Cowboys, 3:17 left to play.

Our offense couldn't move the ball and Air Force takes over with two minutes left. McGee drops Baxter for a nine-yard loss and linebacker Brent Engleright, one of the hardest hitters on the team, follows with a 10-yard sack of his own. But Baxter wasn't finished until his fourth down bomb is knocked away from Longnecker by Mike Newton! Folks…THAT was a ball game…and a 27-25 win for us 'Pokes. Time to celebrate!

Now, when it comes to celebrating…those boys out west can hang with the best and it goes far beyond your basic line dances. I'm not sure if this happened immediately after the win over Air Force, but someone house sitting outside of Laramie decided to throw a party. Among the attendees were quite a few team members. Those of us who were Black, thought it would be good to attend, thinking it was a great opportunity to promote some unity.

I don't really know how it started, but a huge fight broke out. I heard some dudes from Notre Dame had taken a liking to some of the girl friends of the White players. Fists started flying inside the house, and quickly the disturbance traveled out to the snow covered front yard… which was quickly turning red from all the spilled blood. I had never seen anything like it! The house was wrecked. Not one punch was thrown by any of the Black players. But at our next practice, we were told all of us would be held responsible and punished as a group. It became a reflective---could've, would've, should've moment for me. Next time…just stay home.

Gaining Confidence

One thing I liked about the Western Athletic Conference was some of the great nick-names given to players. In my opinion it gave the WAC a little swagger, along with some of the numbers individuals were producing. We were about to face one of the best, "The Clutch McCutch"… Aka Lawrence McCutcheon, Colorado State's sensational sophomore running back. 6'1" 210…fast and rugged, as Texans are known to be (that's coming from an Okie). "The Clutch" had just torched Wichita State for 215 yards on the ground. He had our full attention!

CSU wasn't an easy team to play against from a defensive perspective. A lot of misdirection, coming from all angles. You had to be alert. We were. "The Clutch" would leave the game still looking for some yardage on the ground. He was minus for the day and the Rams went down, in this rivalry game, 39 to 3. I got my second Pick 6...from 24 yards out. I give credit to Nels, McGee, and the rest of the "D", because the quarterback was running for his life....the entire game.

"The Clutch" would finish the year just shy of 800 yards on the ground and ten touchdowns. He would go over 1,000 yards in each of the next two seasons and be drafted in the 3rd round by the Los Angeles Rams. McCutcheon would gain over 6,000 yards rushing during his NFL career and score 26 touchdowns, while setting many records along the way. He became the Rams Director of Player Personnel in 2003. His son Daylon, a cornerback out of USC, played for the Cleveland Browns for eight seasons.

Next up...The University of Texas at El Paso, better known as UTEP. They had a player who had been dubbed "Sonic Boom," and for good reason. Wide receiver Clyde Glosson was a world-class sprinter. A legit 10.23 in the 100 meters. A blur coming out of the slot position. You can probably guess who had responsibility for this potential game breaker. But the night before, a snowstorm hit Laramie. It may not have been as cold as the famous 1967 "ice bowl" game between Green Bay and Dallas (-13 below for that NFC championship game) but it was COLD, as many a warm weather Miner let me know. There was enough snow that the plows had to be brought out to clear the field before the game. I truly didn't think we would play. But we did, much to the dismay of UTEP and "Sonic Boom." 37-9, Cowboys the final.

We started to peek at the polls...and saw that the country was beginning to take notice. United Press International had us ranked 12th and I believe we were 16th in the Associated Press. There was talk that the Sugar Bowl was already looking in our direction for a New Year's Day appearance (there were only 11 bowls in '69). In my opinion, and with apologies to Utah and its outstanding defensive back Norm Thompson, I thought Arizona State and Houston, with receiver Elmo

Wright, would probably offer us the stiffest challenge. The season was still evolving and frankly, I didn't know much about Utah.

It was all just speculation anyway and wouldn't mean a thing in a week…because on the horizon, there was a storm brewing that still affects the state of Wyoming and its beloved Cowboys today. We would be kicked off the team, ending most of our football careers and in the process, ignite a controversy that is still news worthy five decades later.

Unbeknownst to BYU, it would serve as the lightning rod. The Cougars were next on our schedule and the explosion of the Black 14 incident which preceded the game.

After their 40-7 win over BYU, the Cowboys were greeted by armbands worn by the San Jose State football team as a show of support for us! Wyoming would win the game 16-7, but it would be the last victory of the year. The team ended the season with four straight losses. Arizona State scored a 30-14 win, Utah 34-10, New Mexico 24-12, and Houston 41-14. Receiver Elmo Wright, a future first-round pick of the Kansas City Chiefs, was quoted as saying it was the first game he went completely untouched. He scored four touchdowns. Wyoming ended its season of such promise with a 6 and 4 record.

CHAPTER 4

If First You Don't Succeed...

THE CHILL OF THE AUTUMN wind had been replaced by the white stuff rolling off the Laramie Mountains. Down below…the Black 14 situation was heating up and headed for federal court. Attorney William Waterman of Detroit was dispatched by the National Association for the Advancement of Colored People to file a lawsuit on behalf of The Black 14. Waterman was hoping to get an injunction ordering the reinstatement of us and sought damages for violation of our civil rights. He was asking for 1.1 million dollars. That figure was arrived at by our collective minimum potential earnings in the National Football League.

But the injunction was denied by U.S. District Judge Ewing T. Kerr. The same judge who was presiding over our lawsuit against the state and university, was a special guest of the Cheyenne Quarterback Club, during "Cowboy Night." A night when Head Coach Lloyd Eaton, his staff, and his senior players were being honored.

Five months later, Kerr threw our case out of court after a hearing, but without a trial. The 10th Circuit Court of Appeals reversed that decision on May 14, 1971, but after a trial this time, Kerr again ruled for the state on October 18, 1971. The appeals court eventually affirmed him. During the hearing before his first dismissal, Kerr rejected the assertion by Weston Reeves, a Cheyenne attorney also representing us, that the issue of race ran through the case.

"From my observation of almost half a century in Wyoming," Kerr said at the hearing, "I have never known of any prejudice against any race in the state of Wyoming and I think the fact that the Coach went out and solicited and gave scholarships to a large number of colored people is strong evidence that he was not prejudiced against any race."

During the trial…Mel Hamilton, one of the 14, testified that he never told trustees he would not play against BYU without an armband. I told the Laramie Boomerang, the city newspaper, that I wore an armband not because of Mormon beliefs and practices, but because of what some of my Black teammates were saying about mistreatment at Provo the previous season. We wanted to play BYU in the worst kind of way and I saw Eaton as a starting point for negotiations. But after his tirade…he kicked us off the team.

In a Sports Illustrated article following the BYU game, Eaton claimed he had given us ten minutes to speak. Three years later, during the court hearing, Eaton admitted there was no discussion. "They had already violated our coaching rule. There was no purpose in talking."

Here is the condensed ruling by the 10th Circuit Court of Appeals:

"That taking all of the evidence and facts adduced by the parties into consideration, the Court finds that there is no merit in the contention raised by the Plaintiffs in their complaint filed herein that one of the purposes of the black armband display was that of protesting against the alleged cheap shots and name-calling charged to members of the Brigham Young University football team; on the contrary, the Court finds that such allegation is without merit and the sole and only purpose in the armband display was that of protesting against alleged religious beliefs of the Church of Jesus Christ of Latter-day Saints, commonly known as the Mormon Church, and Brigham Young University, which the Plaintiffs considered one and the same, and the Court further finds that each of the Plaintiff football players refused to participate in the football game with Brigham Young University as members of the football team of The University of Wyoming unless they were permitted to demonstrate against

the religious beliefs of the Mormon Church by wearing black armbands upon the playing field.

That, taking all of the evidence and facts adduced by the parties into consideration, the Court finds that each Plaintiffs refused to play football as a member of the University of Wyoming football team unless and until the defendant, Lloyd Eaton, was removed from position as Head Football Coach of The University of Wyoming."

Wow! In other words…they didn't hear our testimony, decided to disregard it, not believe it…or all of the above! But consider this: Why would I, as a 19 year old student athlete, who was enjoying an incredible year, in my first varsity season and a starter as a sophomore, on a highly ranked team that could end up in a major bowl game, put everything in jeopardy…because of someone else's religious beliefs? (As of this printing…50 years after The Black 14 incident, and after only four games, that produced two interception returns for touchdowns, Jerry Berry is listed in two categories in the Wyoming football record book…along with three other players for Total Interceptions Returned For Touchdowns in a career. And tied with two other players for a single season.)

Why would I, who knew nothing about the Mormon religion, before enrolling at the University of Wyoming and who, as a freshman, entertained an offer to spend the Christmas holidays with a teammate who was a Mormon…suddenly feel so differently?

Why would I, a product of a single parent home…and who's extended family had produced only one college graduate, decide that this issue was worth sacrificing everything I had worked for? The answer is simple…I wouldn't! I wanted to ask my coach some questions and was found guilty for wanting to do it!

This, in the "Equality State," which is Wyoming's nickname. Actually, this can be a bit misleading because the title deals with women being able to vote. Wyoming was the first state to grant it in 1869. In addition, women were allowed to serve on juries and hold public office. Oddly enough, the move giving women the right to vote in Wyoming evolved mainly because of the 14th and 15th amendments to the Constitution. The 14th Amendment guarantees that former slaves would be citizens, protected by the law like anyone else. The 15th Amendment guarantees that no people could be denied the right to vote based on their color or on the fact that they had once been slaves.

Early Wyoming politicians were looking for some good publicity and more women for the territory. There were six adult men for every adult woman. Black men and Chinese were included in that number. Democrats, who held the majority of seats in the legislature, hoped that once these women came to Wyoming, they would continue to vote for the party that had given them the ability to vote in the first place and negate the votes of ex-slaves. After learning this…the nickname "Equality State" might not carry the same meaning as it once did. I know it's changed for me, in more ways than one.

WHERE DO WE GO FROM HERE?

With no college and no team, my future wasn't easy to interpret. I was starting from ground zero, that's for sure, and time was an enemy. There was encouraging talk that big time programs like USC were interested in my talents, but rumor is all that turned out to be. In reality the war in Vietnam was the only sure thing to consider and that wasn't very appealing.

Transferring schools could mean the loss of college credits…and my deferment from the draft. We were considered to be rabble rousers, and Black Power advocates, not the kind of people you want on your team. It turns out that even Grambling and Morgan State, the Black colleges that Eaton suggested we attend, weren't beating down our doors, wanting to bring us on-board…hardly.

Three of the Black 14, wide receiver John Griffin, running back Ted Williams, and defensive lineman Don Meadows returned to the Cowboys but their futures didn't hold any guarantees. The team's cupboard was lacking players and talent, and it showed, as it lost every home game...and all but the Colorado State contest during the 1970 season. The one-win, nine-loss campaign was the worst record since 1939, and the first time Wyoming had lost all its home games since 1931 and since we're keeping count, it's the first losing season for the Cowboys since 1948.

Eaton was planning to rejuvenate his program by stepping up recruiting, particularly from the junior college ranks. But the university had other plans and announced Eaton was "retiring" from active coaching and concentrating on becoming an assistant athletic director, whose duties were still undetermined.

Eaton's goal was to succeed Red Jacoby as athletic director after Jacoby's retirement. It didn't happen. In 1972 Eaton became the Director of Player Personnel for the Green Bay Packers, before being demoted to a scouting position four years later. He died in 2007 at the age of 88.

During a 1982 interview with the Denver Post newspaper, Eaton was asked if he had to do it again, would he do anything differently. "It was a very easy decision to make, and I'd make it again." Bo Schembechler, the late, former University of Michigan head coach used to ask me continuously..."Berry, what was he thinking?" My response was pretty much always the same, Coach, I have no clue! 1969 was Schembechler's first year as the Wolverine's head coach.

Fritz Shurmur, Wyoming's defensive coordinator, was faced with the unenviable task of trying to right the Cowboys' sinking ship when he became the teams' head coach in 1971. His squads went 15 and 29 during his four seasons. Wyoming had only one winning season in the '70's, as the Black 14 incident plagued the team for years to come. The Cowboys didn't return to a bowl game until the 1976 Fiesta Bowl.

In 1978, spurred on by demonstrations and worldwide challenges regarding racial issues, The Church of Jesus Christ of Latter-day Saints rescinded the restriction on priesthood ordination, meaning all Blacks who are worthy, could become priest. It also extended the blessings of the temple to all worthy latter-day Saints, men and women.

40 years later, the Church of Jesus Christ of Ladder-day Saints celebrated this anniversary, a racial milestone...a celebration of Black Mormon. It was a featured story on a national NBC news broadcast July 8, 2018. The spotlight was literally on its most recognizable Black member, rhythm and blues icon Gladys Knight, who performed from the pulpit the song "Somewhere" from the 1957 Broadway musical "Westside Story" by Leonard Bernstein and lyrics by Stephen Sondheim:

"There's a time for us, Time together with time to spare,
Time to look, time to care,
Someday! Somewhere.
We'll find a new way of living,
we'll find a way of forgiving
somewhere.
There's a place for us, a time and place for us.
Hold my hand and I'll take you there.
Somehow.
Someday.
Somewhere!"

Today, according to the news report...of the more than six million Mormons, less than two percent are Black and have yet to break through the Church's highest ranks of leadership, and inclusion in racial sensitivity is still a struggle. Yet, or maybe because of it, the Church of Jesus Christ of Ladder-Saints has reportedly forged an alliance with the National Association for the Advancement of Colored People. According to Dallin Oaks, the LDS Church President, "Most in the Church, including its senior leadership, have concentrated on the opportunities of the future, rather than the disappointments of the past."

I couldn't help but wonder if: the University of Wyoming, its trustees, its governor, its legislature, and representatives of its court system were listening. 14 athletes, who were verbally abused with the most contemptible racial language, ridiculed, and the targets of continuous fabrications for half a century...still look for justice from a state that used our considerable talents and skills, before casting us away like yesterday's garbage!

Wyoming Tri-captain Joe Williams was a 12th round selection of the Dallas Cowboys in1970. He won a Super Bowl with the team in 1971. Joe, a running back, also played for the New Orleans Saints.

A.E. (Tony) McGee, was a 3rd round draft choice of the Chicago Bears. He was projected as a first rounder, before it was learned he was a member of the Black 14. McGee, a defensive end, made two Super Bowl appearances with the Washington Redskins and won a ring in 1983.

Ivie Moore and John Griffin say they suited up for Winnipeg in the Canadian Football League (CFL), but were not teammates.

1969 was the end of the football careers for Black 14 members Lionel Grimes, Earl Lee, Mel Hamilton, Ron Hill, Guillermo (Willie) Hysaw, Tony Gibson, and yours truly.

James Issac, Lee and Meadows are no longer with us. Issac, a defensive back from Hanna, Wyoming continued his football career and ran track at Dakota Wesleyan University in South Dakota. He earned a degree from there as well. Issac died in 1976 following a dispute with his wife.

Earl Lee, an offensive guard from Chattanooga, Tennessee had a distinguished career as a teacher, coach and principal in the Baltimore, Maryland area. He passed away in 2013 from heart disease.

Don Meadows, a middle guard from Denver, was selected to the All-Western Athletic Conference first team his senior year. His brother Mel, a defensive back, would join him at the University of Wyoming. Don had a restaurant business in Denver. He passed away in 2009.

Alsuma, Oklahoma..early 50's. That's me on the left. Faceless, but that would change.

School Days
1959-1960

Orange Bowl Trip Payoff for Champions.

That's me top row, fifth from left.

1967 FOOTBALL RECORD

Hornets	33	East Central	6
Hornets	56	Webster	0
Hornets	34	Muskogee Manual	0
Hornets	53	Bartlesville Sooner	0
Hornets	49	McLain	0
Hornets	28	McAlester	0
Hornets	31	Oklahoma City Douglass	0
Hornets	26	Memorial	0
Hornets	21	Sapulpa	6
Hornets	35	Ponca City	0
Hornets	30	Midwest City	14

Won 11, Lost 0

I was honored to serve as Student Council President

Mr. Hornet XI
Jerome Berry

*Wyoming team pic.

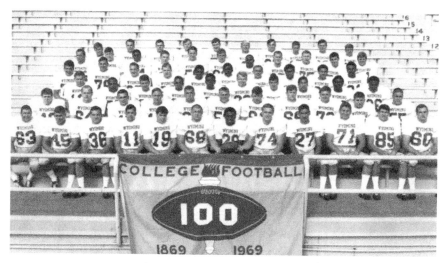

That's me, fourth row...far right.

Working to be the best!

WYOMING SAFETY Jerry Berry (21) intercepts a Brian Linstrom pass intended for Arizona halfback Ron Gardin (22) and rambles 88 yards for a touchdown Saturday in Wyoming's 23-7 win over the Wildcats in Laramie. Linebacker Brent Engleright (45) and middle guard Steve Adamson (63) are shown in the third quarter action. **(UPI Photo)**

Pick six! 88 yards later...touchdown!

UPI Football Ratings
(Won-lost-tied record, first-place votes in parentheses)

Team	Points
1. Ohio State (33) (3-0)	346
2. Texas (2) (4-0)	292
3. USC (4-0)	238
4. Penn State (4-0)	204
5. Missouri (4-0)	196
6. Arkansas (4-0)	173
7. Tennessee (4-0)	118
8. UCLA (5-0)	111
9. LSU (4-0)	98
10. Notre Dame (3-1)	32
11. Oklahoma (2-1)	31
12. Wyoming (4-0)	22
13. Florida (4-0)	21
14. (tie) Georgia (3-1)	12
(tie) Michigan (3-1)	12
16. Kansas State (3-1)	7
17. (tie) Auburn (3-1)	3
(tie) California (3-1)	3
19. (tie) Purdue (3-1)	1
(tie) Mississippi (2-2)	1
(tie) Stanford (2-2)	1
(tie) Colorado (2-2)	1

Rising in the polls! Number 12 and undefeated!

14 Negro Football Players Booted For Armbands

Negroes Protest Intelligence Tests

The Black 14 incident explodes!

Sports Illustrated Article.

Jet Magazine gets the word out.

KLEY, W. VA., MONDAY MORNING, OCTOBER 20, 1969

At University Of Wyoming

Dismissal Of 14 Gridders May Effect Other Sports

LARAMIE, Wyo. (AP) — The dismissal Friday of 14 players from the University of Wyoming football team showed evidence Sunday of effecting splits in both the basketball and track teams also.

The protest leading to the dismissals involved the racial policies of the Mormon Church and its related Brigham Young University. Widespread demonstrations of support for Coach Lloyd Eaton and his decision, with player-coach loyalty and rule-breaking at issue.

Kicker Bob Jacobs, a white member of the football team said in an interview that the dismissals worked as a "reverse psych"—making the remainder of the squad "win more" for Eaton.

Tackle Frosty Franklin echoed Jacobs' opinion when asked if he thought the Cowboys, minus 14, could successfully defend their Western Athletic Conference championship: "I really don't know but we're trying harder than ever for the coach."

Eaton says the players violated his rule that nobody on the Cowboys' squad could participate in a student demonstration. Willie S. Black, chancellor of the campus Black Student Alliance (BSA) said Sunday, "This means when you become an athlete on Eaton's team your right to protest is abrogated."

Questioning of other students on campus the day after Wyoming whipped Brigham Young 40-7 revealed that most of them seem to feel Eaton took the only steps he could, because they feel the blacks broke the rules.

Black said the case may end up in court as a civil rights action but first the BSA would try to marshal faculty and student action to reverse Eaton's decision.

Eaton dismissed them Friday morning after they appeared in his office wearing black armbands. Such armbands had been worn by campus blacks for several days in protest of the BYU game. Similar protests have occurred at least six times prior to other BYU games at other schools.

The blacks said they were protesting the policies of the Church of Jesus Christ of the Latter-day Saints — Mormons—which they say limits Negro advancement in the church hierarchy.

The Student Senate Saturday censured the university trustees' upholding Eaton in an emergency meeting Friday with Gov. Stan Hathaway present. The student leaders also voted to freeze student funds allocated to athletics.

The existence of an anti-demonstrations rule is disputed here. White players on the team Sunday agreed with the BSA that there was no such rule.

Eaton stayed isolated from the press, a spokesman said stating that the coach was reviewing game films.

Track Coach John Walker reported: "Friday night a spokesman for the eight black members of the track team called and made an appointment with me. Huey Johnson (defending WAC 440-yard champion) was the spokesman, and he said, "We want to let you know how we feel about the thing with the football team. If they quit, we'll be going along with them."

Walker said he would try to help anyone who wanted to stay, to continue his education and to compete. But then, the coach said, "One of the eight started to 'smart off' and I told them all to go outside and come back one by one if they wanted to stay on the team." He said they all left and none came back.

SUCCESSFUL DEBUT --
ALEX WEBSTER, NEW HEAD COACH OF THE NEW YORK GIANTS, MADE A SUCCESSFUL DEBUT A WEEK AFTER GETTING THE JOB, AS HE TRIES TO END THE CLUBS LONGEST STRING OF NON-WINNING SEASONS.
Distributed by King Features

Fairmont Leads WVC Standings

BECKLEY (AP) — Fairmont State's football Falcons lost their first game of the season last weekend but continue to hold a tight lead in the West Virginia Intercollegiate Athletic Conference ratings.

WVIAC Commissioner George Springer, who released the ratings Sunday, gave Fairmont 123.3 ratings points for its 3-0 conference record.

Salem College was in second place with 98 points and a 4-1 WVIAC record with West Liberty third and West Virginia State dropping into fourth place.

Fairmont dropped a 20-13 decision to Hillsdale College of Michigan while the other top teams won their games.

Here are the WVIAC football ratings with conference records in parenthesis and overall records:

1. Fairmont (3-0) 123.3 3-1
2. Salem (4-1) 98.0 4-1
4. West Liberty (4-1) 83.5 4-2
4. W.Va. State (3-1) 82.5 3-1
5. Glenville (2-2) 57.5 2-3
6. Shepherd (1-1) 26.0 3-1
7. Bluefield State (2-3) .. 42.0 2-4
8. W.Va. Wesleyan (1-4) .. 22.0 1-4
9. W.Va. Tech (1-4) 20.0 1-5
10. Concord (0-4) 0.0 0-5

Penn State, Florida, Texas Win

Three black trackmen leave campus

POST-GAZETTE: Fri., May 14, 1982—17

No regrets, says Eaton 13 years after 'crash'

By The Associated Press

Lloyd Eaton, whose highly successful college football coaching career crumbled after he kicked 14 black players off the University of Wyoming team 13 years ago, says he still has no regrets.

"Hell, no. Not once," Eaton said in a recent interview with the Denver Post, when asked if he has had any second thoughts about the decision that rocked Wyoming and left the school with a football program that didn't produce another winning Cowboys team for seven years.

Eaton, now 64, is a scout for the Green Bay Packers of the National Football League.

The incident that prompted what became known as the "Black 14" occurred on the morning of Oct. 17, 1969 — a Friday — when the 14 black players showed up in Eaton's office wearing black armbands.

They had come, they said later, to seek Eaton's permission to wear the armbands the next day in a home game against Brigham Young University. They said they wanted to protest what they considered the racist policies of the Church of the Latter-day Saints — policies that at that time kept blacks from becoming Mormon priests.

The players said they never had a chance to voice their concern or make their request. Eaton simply kicked them off the team — enforcing his standing rule against players demonstrating or protesting in any way.

Eaton said in the interview that if he were coaching today, he would have reacted the same way. "They were biting the hand that feeds them," he said. "It was an affront to all of athletics. It was a very easy decision to make, and I'd make it again."

Eaton was asked what he would do if he met one of the members of the "Black 14" on the street today. "I probably wouldn't recognize him," Eaton said. "He'd probably have a mustache and long hair and everything."

Some of the players harbor similar feelings of bitterness.

Mel Hamilton, a tackle who now is an executive for an oil drilling company in Casper, Wyo., was asked what his reaction would be if he met Eaton today. Said Hamilton, "I'd tell him, 'You're the best coach I've ever had. But as far as a human being, you ain't worth a damn.'"

Earl Lee, a guard who now is a football coach and biology teacher at a Baltimore high school, said, "I'd say, 'It takes a long time to build an empire, coach, but you found out just how quick you can tear it down.'"

Safety Jerry Berry, now a weekend sports television anchorman in Chicago, said, "I'd tell him all we wanted to do was talk to him. We just wanted to talk. We would have played anyway (against BYU). A lot of lives were changed because he wouldn't listen. It's too bad."

At the time of the incident, Wyoming was 4-0, ranked in the top 10 nationally, was considered a near shoo-in for a major bowl game, and had posted a 31-5 record in the previous 3½ seasons under Eaton.

Even without the black players, Wyoming smashed BYU, 40-7, and beat San Jose State the following weekend.

But that was the end. Wyoming lost its last four games in 1969, went 1-9 the following year and, unable to recruit blacks for several years after the incident, didn't produce a winner until current Texas Coach Fred Akers led Wyoming to the Western Athletic Conference title, a Fiesta Bowl appearance and an 8-4 record in 1976.

Eaton, whose overall record at Wyoming in nine years as head coach was 57-33-2, was moved to assistant athletic director after his 1-9 season but was stripped of his coaching duties. In 1972 he was named director of player personnel for the Packers. In 1978, he was demoted to a scout.

Eaton said he believes that the rumors which circulated in 1969 that the "Black 14" were influenced by outside radical groups. "It was nothing but a big show deal," he said. "Fourteen kids are not going to think all that up themselves.

"If they were so serious about their grievance, why didn't they all go to the Mormon church directly? Why did they have to pick on the University of Wyoming? Why didn't they do that instead of giving athletes a bad eye?"

Thirteen of the "Black 14" are alive. Halfback Jim Isaac was shot to death by his wife on Christmas Eve 1976.

Three of them came back in 1970 to play for Eaton — split end John Griffin, middle guard Don Meadows and tailback Ted Williams.

Three others wound up at colleges that were then all-black — defensive end Tony McGee and Berry at Bishop College in Dallas and split end Ron Hill at Howard University in Washington, D.C.

None of the 14 was able to transfer to a major university. "We were what I call 'whiteballed,'" said flanker Willie Hysaw, now coordinator of sales promotion for the Pontiac Division of General Motors in Pontiac, Mich. "Colleges that had shown a lot of interest in us in high school weren't interested anymore. They thought we were troublemakers."

Two of the "Black 14" went on to the National Football League. McGee still plays for the New England Patriots, and tailback Joe Williams played for four years with Dallas, New Orleans and the Los Angeles Rams.

CHAPTER 5

Turn Your TV On T-Town!

I PLANNED ON CONTINUING MY football career... just as McGee did. In fact for a semester we were teammates again, at Bishop College down in Dallas, Texas. It was a historically Black college, founded by the Baptist Home Mission Society in 1881. It wasn't WAC competition...but SWAC, The Southwestern Athletic Conference. Grambling, Jackson State, Southern University, Alcorn State, and Texas Southern were among the teams in the Conference. My former coach at Booker T., Robert Mayes, came to my rescue. He had a contact at Bishop. I told Coach Mayes about Tony, and he said bring him too. I can't tell you the level of relief I felt. But anxiety was knocking on my door before I could even settle in Big D.

I was being ordered to take a physical for the military. The Vietnam War wasn't going away, in fact it was expanding into Cambodia...thus increasing my chances of being caught up in it, if I lost my student deferment. It appeared to me someone in Wyoming, with ties to the draft board, was keeping a close eye on me. I was supposed to take the physical in Denver, but I explained to the officials I was headed to Dallas, so it was delayed until my arrival there.

I knew my chances of avoiding the draft were slim to none and as the joke goes, "Slim just left town." My draft number was 42 or 43, which ever it was, it all but sealed my fate since numbers well into the 200's were being selected!

I was worried sick, but come to think of it...that may have worked in my favor. The Vietnam War was unpopular to say the least. It polarized our nation like never before and was actually set into motion way back in 1950, with the arrival of American military advisors in what was then French Indochina. France, with financial assistance from the United States, was involved in an armed struggle with the North Vietnamese and National Liberation Front, who were motivated to fight because of significant social changes in post World War Two Vietnam.

South Vietnam viewed it as a civil war, a defensive war against communism or a need to protect their homes, families, and way of life. The U.S. government became involved to prevent a communist takeover of South Vietnam. Many more factions were also fighting, including not surprisingly, the Soviet Union and China who supported the North Vietnamese. In addition to the United States and France, the South Vietnamese were backed by South Korea, Australia, Thailand, and other anti-communist allies.

For many Americans, there was no clear cut reason for our involvement outside of the threat of communism and while that was a unifying cause, the rising death total had many questioning the conflict. In addition, civil unrest in America and social issues were mounting reasons to end the war, plus there was a growing suspicion that our politicians and military leaders were not being completely honest about their intentions...and the results of the fighting.

That kind of setting didn't have young men rushing to sign up to do battle. But the draft took care of that. Virtually all male U.S. citizens, regardless of where they live, and male immigrants, whether documented or undocumented, residing in the United States, who are 18 through 25...are required to register with Selective Service within 30 days of their 18th birthday, it's the law. But this does not mean you are joining the military, however in 1970 and because of the Vietnam War, chances of you putting on a uniform were pretty good.

So there I was in Dallas, stripped down to my underwear and pretending I couldn't hear. The examining official had surely seen this before and he was in no mood for my games. "You know you hear that!" Huh, what did you say?

Even before arriving to take the physical, some guys had done just about everything they could think of to appear physically unfit. Some even claimed to have eaten soap! What would that do (besides kill you?) I'm not sure, but it wouldn't be good! Desperate times…desperate measures. So imagine my surprise when I was told to step out of the line of potential inductees and pointed to another part of the room. Go wait over there, someone will see you in a moment, I was told.

Now what? I'm racking my brain trying to figure out what this was all about? Had I angered the physician that much during the ear test? On top of that, I was the only one in this waiting area. When I was approached, the man looked as if he had suffered a major loss or something. With sincere eyes and demeanor, he looked at me and said he was sorry…."we can't use you." What? Can't use me? Is he saying what I think he is saying? He said, "You have high blood pressure." High blood pressure?

I've never been diagnosed with this before. A few months ago, I was playing major college football, enduring strenuous workouts in an extremely high altitude environment, never taking oxygen, with no complaints about my health…and in the best shape of my life. Now the armed services say they can't use me, because of high blood pressure? Thank you Jesus! More tests will have to follow, over a period of time I'm told…but "from the numbers we're looking at, you're not fit for military service."

I walk out of there in a daze. I wanted to jump for joy, clap my hands and dance down the street. Then I probably would have been locked up in a mental institution or some place that resembled one. Was it all that drama we went through because of the Black 14 incident? Was it the altitude? This just didn't make sense. So many of my friends who went to 'Nam…never returned. Millions were killed, maimed, and had their lives destroyed because they were not the same person as when they left. Why me? Why am I being spared?

The Vietnam War lasted 19 years. All air-force and naval units and all other forces were completely withdrawn August 15, 1973. The capture of Saigon by the North Vietnamese Army in April 1975 marked the end of the war. North and South Vietnam were reunified the following year.

I was one and done after a semester at Bishop College. The school was fine and I had set up my classes so Thursday evening I could take a bus to Tulsa and return on Sunday. The 250 mile trip took roughly 4 ½ hours. The racial situation was just the opposite from what I experienced in Laramie. Plenty of Black folks to go around and some of them, like quarterback Bo Tiger, were my teammates at Booker T. Washington High School. That was a major plus!

My problem at Bishop dealt with one of my new coaches. He would ask why I didn't "stick" with my people in the first place, instead of going to Wyoming. It felt like discrimination in the reverse and after what happened with the Cowboys, I wasn't having it. Tony McGee stayed and became an All America. He even played with the College All Stars who faced the NFL Champs in Chicago and was drafted by the Bears. McGee would also play with the New England Patriots and go to two Super Bowls with the Washington Redskins. They won it all in '83. "Mac the Sack" as McGee was called, recorded 96.5 sacks during his 14 year career and was a source of pride for the rest of the Black 14, who lived vicariously through his successes in the National Football League.

Hanging up the Cleats

Tell someone you're from Oklahoma and you can almost see a tumble weed blow through their thoughts. "That dust bowl, what's it like?" In reality I'm from Tulsa, the heart of Green Country, which practically kisses the rolling hills of the Ozarks. My hometown is a little taste of the city and the country at the same time…with familiar faces and places, like Warren Petroleum, where I worked summers after high school. In the 60's, Warren Petroleum was one of many oil companies that helped Tulsa maintain its status of Oil Capitol of the World, until Houston claimed the title. Warren handled the gas and gas liquids for Gulf Oil and was eventually bought out by the huge corporation.

I was one of the students who benefited from programs that introduced us to the oil business and some of its inner workings. Part of this process allowed young adults, who were headed off to college, to be placed in departments like accounting and marketing...which helped further our goals of becoming future business leaders. I always wanted to have more going for me than just athletics. It was part of my "plan" way back in junior high school to be the best on the field and courts...and in the classroom too. The summer jobs generally had us working in the department offices upstairs. Now that I was back and full time, I was starting literally at the bottom, in the mailroom. There were about half a dozen of us...working and going to school at night. Warren Petroleum reimbursed us for fifty percent of our tuition and added other incentives to encourage us. Not a bad gig, because in addition to all of that, they hired from within the company. If a job opened upstairs, we generally had the first shot at getting it.

But my transition from the football field wasn't as seamless as it appeared outwardly. I couldn't watch college football. It hurt too much, seeing people I both played with or against...and know that I was just as good, if not better. Fortunately for me, my stepfather Claude liked fishing about as much as he liked cooking. We both immersed ourselves into the art of bass fishing...and it is an art if you want to be good at it. How do you maneuver a plastic worm or crank bait? What colors or depths work best? How about your speed? Hey, this is serious stuff and a lot of fun. We also would go below Keystone dam and bounce jigs off the rocks and catch big sand bass, stripers, and channel catfish.

This occupied me for a while, but I was lured back to the football field, this time as a coach. I reconnected with some of my high school teammates and began sharing what I knew with the players at Carver Junior High School. This is where I needed to be and we had some good teams. We would, if possible, start our practices by reaching out to the kids. Find out what was going on in their lives and what may be troubling them. It's a good way to connect. You learn much more about them...and them about you. It reminded me of years ago when somebody got my attention and steered me in the right direction. These days it's called giving back.

The players were skilled...but like most of us at this age, have to be taught technique, tendencies to look out for, and how to be disciplined. Everybody wants to be a star but how do you handle success or failure? On a few occasions to prove a point...or that I meant business, I would bench a starter and pick a third stringer, who has shown up every day, and on time...and insert him into the starting lineup. Now I have their attention! It was very satisfying to see someone "buy in" to what I was trying to sell him and then see him rewarded. That's what it's all about!

The players wore those purple and white colors proudly, and would do the same at B.T.W. sporting the orange, black and white. They represented themselves with distinction, both in their athletic pursuits, and often in the classroom. GO CATS!

While coaching there, we won more than our share of conference championships at Carver....but we were expected to do that. However, I received just as much satisfaction, if not more, coaching a season at Immaculate Conception...a private school in the area.

I felt conflicted going there, but it was a challenge I welcomed. The players were willing...however they didn't know what it would take to be successful, just how much they would have to give of themselves... to succeed. First of all, I had to restrict mommy and daddy from coming to the practices. That way, when little Johnnie complained about his hands hurting because he thought a pass was thrown too hard, he couldn't run over to the sidelines and be comforted. There is no coddling on the football field!

It took us a while, but the end of the season looked a lot different than the beginning. Games in which we were getting blown out earlier, now were reversed, and turned into runaway victories. Little Johnnie couldn't believe it and neither could mommy or daddy! We had a lot of fun...eventually.

I have settled into my new norm…working, going to school and giving back to North Tulsa, the same way it was done for me years ago. But I have learned, if I'm paying attention and willing to pay a price as well…God can lead me to places and opportunities I could never dream or imagine!

Knock, Knock…it's the NFL

January 17, 1973…before the annual NFL draft, I receive a letter from the Dallas Cowboys! I had not been contacted by or involved with anyone regarding football outside of my junior high coaching jobs. Again, it's one of those moments when I shake my head and say……. how could this be happening?

> *Dear Jerome:*
> *We would like you to know that after a very thorough analyzation of the nation's college football talent, we are considering you as one of our choices for the National Football League draft which is being held January 30th.*
> *We have compiled this booklet with the hope of answering any questions you may have about the National Football League or Dallas and the Cowboys. If you have any additional questions, we would be very happy to hear from you.*
>
> *Would you please complete the enclosed form and return as soon as possible. It is of UTMOST IMPORTANCE to have this additional information on record so you may be located during that time in regards to your being drafted.*
>
> *Sincerely yours,*
> *DALLAS COWBOYS FOOTBALL CLUB*
>
> *Gil Brandt*
> *Vice President*

The Dallas Cowboys! Since Oklahoma didn't have an NFL franchise, it was the team I followed. You have to understand, pro football players were larger than life to me.

Most of my time getting a college scholarship had all my attention. There weren't any thoughts of me one day being able to play as a pro. Although with my early success at the University of Wyoming, I was beginning to think I might be good enough for the NFL. Still, I wasn't sure…after all, my college career had just begun before being quickly terminated. This was too much to comprehend!

My head is spinning…and the numbers related to my high blood pressure, had to be off the charts! I hadn't played football since I left Laramie over three years before…and then, it was for just four varsity games! If there had not been other documents sent with the letter, with the Dallas Cowboys logo, I might have thought this was some kind of cruel joke. But wait there's more. Six days after being contacted by Dallas I receive another letter, this time from the St. Louis Cardinals! I am totally blown away and feeling conflicted.

Dear Mr. Berry:
The St. Louis Football Cardinals are interested in learning more about you. We are enclosing a questionnaire which we would appreciate you filling out and returning to us in the self-addressed envelope. This questionnaire will assist us in our total evaluation of your abilities in relation to our present squad.

We will be back in touch with you, if we feel it will be mutually beneficial for you and the Cardinals.

Thank you in advance for an early response.
Sincerely yours,
ST. LOUIS FOOTBALL CARDINALS

E.R. "ABE" STUBER
Director of Player Personnel

Wow! I'm thinking, is this really happening? I don't remember filling out the forms for the Cardinals, but I don't believe I wouldn't have. Dallas followed up, and informed me they were sending a scout to the University of Tulsa to check on some players there. They wanted me to join the workouts. 1973 was the year Drew Pearson signed as a free agent out of Tulsa. He of course went on to become an incredible pro...and Roger Staubach's "go to" target at wide receiver.

Dallas would draft Drane Scrivener, a safety and former running back, out of the University of Tulsa in the fourth round. If I recall correctly, he had some medical issues and didn't play in the pros. As for my own situation, the high blood pressure was controlled with medication. However, trying to get my body ready for the workout proved to be too much for my back. I was in no shape to compete, which was no surprise, considering how long I had been away from the game. I was given encouragement from the Dallas scout, to get in shape and come to camp as a free agent.

I considered it, but realized it wouldn't be the best move for me. My oldest daughter was just a year old. Considering my opportunities at Warren Petroleum, that path appeared to be more of a sure thing. Money I could take to the bank. Timing, as they say is everything, but my time had come and gone for my football playing days. However, God still had something in store for me and He wouldn't take long to reveal it.

Lights, Action...Camera

My years as a coach came to a screeching halt when I bumped into John Thiel one day. John, an Advertising Analyst at Warren Petroleum, told me he just left a meeting with Tom Goodgame, the Vice President and General Manager for KTUL-TV, Channel 8 in Tulsa. John said Mr. Goodgame informed him that he was looking to expand his sports department and John said he thought of me. John told me I should give Mr. Goodgame a call. John was a nice man and our conversations were always pleasant, but they didn't go any further than that. I had no idea he thought of me beyond work…and now he's just delivered this incredible news. Try to convince me that there is no God!

I caught my breath, collected my thoughts, and tried to imagine how this all would turn out? I contacted Mr. Goodgame and set up a meeting. He was businesslike but approachable. He handed me a piece of paper (copy) and told me to read it, while delivering it into a television camera. I had absolutely no experience in the media, none. But thankfully, my time spent as both my junior high school student council president and the same in high school, had prepared me for this. I thought of my teachers who emphasized pronunciation, enunciation, and how to use my diaphragm while singing in the school choir. With all that going through my mind, I swallowed and began to read.

It wasn't the most compelling story, hardly. In fact it was downright boring and dry. The subject was about some upcoming soccer matches, and a few that had already been played. Like I said, boring! But when I finished, Mr. Goodgame told me he wanted to hire me as his week-end sports anchor. Was I interested? Do kids like candy?

Believe it or not…that is how my career in broadcasting started. But had it not been for the incredibly nice people I worked with at Warren Petroleum, it wouldn't have happened. As I look back on my life and my experiences, I appreciate them even more. People like J.D Hoff, my supervisor in the tax accounting department. He, like John Thiel, had an easy going style…unless he needed to pump out some numbers, then his right hand was flying over that old calculator like you wouldn't believe. He took a real interest in me. It was just the compassion I needed after what happened in Wyoming and showed me, what I already knew, "You can't judge a book by its cover."

Turns out Mr. Goodgame was a similar kind of man. During his tenure, KTUL-TV rose to be the number one ABC station in the country. I'm not sure what that was based on, but I can vouch for Mr. Goodgame, he was an exceptional human being. He left Tulsa in 1980 and joined Westinghouse Broadcasting and was eventually named president of

GROUP W Television. He retired in 1991 and in that same year, was named President Emeritus of Group W.

Mr. Goodgame decided to hire me away from Warren Petroleum. Thanks to him, I became the second African American anchor-reporter on Tulsa television. Dale Hogg, a former Hornet, was the first. Because Dale was working at a competing station, it opened the door for me. This was 1973 and stations around the country were trying to become more diverse. But because they were, didn't mean we didn't have to work to stay in our jobs. It gave me an opportunity and I wanted to make the most of it!

Dale Hogg was also head of the Tulsa Urban League. Later he served in management positions in both the Corporate Communications and Human Resources of the Williams Companies, a Fortune 500 energy company based in Tulsa.

As for me, after having this dream opportunity land literally in my lap, what was I going to do with it? First and foremost…don't blow it! Which was a distinct possibility when you consider I have no experience in television, and the technology that goes with putting a newscast on the air. What about my clothes? My wig (hair)? Mr. Goodgame had another question. "What about your name? What do they call you? Jerome is rather formal for television." Well, my friends call me J.B. I told him. "That's it," he said…"from now on you are Jay Berry!" To this day, if someone calls me Jerome, I know they must really know me.

From North Tulsa, you're heading south, via The L.L. Tisdale Parkway. Connect to I-244 and travel past downtown, which is on your left. Go over the Arkansas River. To your right is a refinery, beyond that is a place called Lookout Mountain. Sitting on top of it…is KTUL-TV, Channel 8…my new home.

I'll admit growing up I was not a big news watcher, how many kids are? But I knew who Cy Tuma was. He was the guy with the big, deep, booming voice delivering the news. Don Woods was the weather man accompanied by his partner…Gusty. Everybody, young or old, knew who Gusty was, even though he wasn't human, or real for that matter. Yet he was arguably one of the biggest attractions for KTUL...and never got paid one red cent. You see, Gusty was the cartoon character Don Woods drew to help illustrate the weather. You knew what kind of day or night was expected by what Gusty was doing or wearing.

I, like the rest of Tulsa, knew who Betty Boyd was, namely the queen of local television. She would later, among other things, serve nine years as a member of the Oklahoma House of Representatives. Then, when I arrived, there was Bob Hower. Great smile, good hair, and movie star looks. The consummate pro and one with a heart and compassion. It was a team I was proud to join.

Jim Holtzman was our news director. He would probably prefer being introduced as a left handed shooting guard from St. Louis. He was a mentor and a friend. Just the person I needed because of my inexperience, and I think he realized it.

The nuts and bolts and beyond, even the way to hold my script papers...he showed me how to do it. If...and that's important to note, if he liked you, which was generally the case...believed in you and what your cause or argument might be...he would forever be in your corner, maybe even to his own detriment.

One case in point, many years after we both left Tulsa, Jim was caught up in a controversial situation involving one of his news anchors, who was arrested and convicted of child-molestation charges. The anchor served three years in prison. During the ordeal Jim never wavered in his support. According to the San Diego Reader, an alternative press paper, "Holtzman almost destroyed his own staff" defending the employee.

Need I tell you his approach to the news was also different? He would sometimes try something unconventional, and if it didn't work, it was on to the next assignment or experiment...or both. He would sometimes miss his mark, but far more than not, he achieved his desired goal.

The Big Z...Steve Zabriskie was KTUL's Sports Director. He had a relaxed way of delivery and a gift of gab, which served him well after

Channel 8. He would become the voice of the New York Mets. He also called games for the Boston Red Sox, Major League Baseball, and ESPN, NFL, and college basketball. Zabriskie also liked to play golf... which helped with my exposure, because I filled in for him.

Our weekend team included Doug McAllister, who offered another helpful hand when needed. Terry Young delivered the weather. Terry would become Tulsa's 33rd mayor...serving in that capacity from 1984-1986. I got the impression Terry wasn't very fond of me. During a "toss" he said "from a low point, to an even lower point, here's Jay with sports." Ouch! For years I took it personally, what did I ever do to him?

I read a 1993 article in the Tulsa World newspaper, "Terry Young: The Man Tulsans Love to Hate." Guess I wasn't the only one he rubbed the wrong way.

I really wasn't as good as I wanted to be on television. Everything was new and EVERYBODY saw my failures. Many a night I wanted to climb into a hole and not emerge for a couple weeks, hoping by then, my last performance had been forgotten!

Like what happened at a golf tournament hosted at Southern Hills Country Club. First of all, African Americans were not allowed to play golf at Southern Hills. You could serve as a waiter or a caddy...but you weren't playing golf on that course. It was not allowed. No excuse, just the truth. That was generally the situation throughout the country.

So golf was not my game. I tried to plead my case when talk of this upcoming tournament was brought up at channel 8. But to no avail! The powers that be wanted to show me off. I was positioned at or near the ninth hole, not knowing a dog leg...from elephant ears. I was seriously focused on seeing the ball in flight and staying with it, until it hit the ground. It was going pretty good, until some white puffy clouds showed up. "Let's go to Jay Berry... out at the 9th and find out more about this approach. Jay?" Uh, well... actually, you can probably see it better than I can!

I was devastated...and could only imagine the reaction all across Tulsa and three neighboring states. That hole I mentioned earlier to escape moments like this? It had grown. Maybe I won't ever show my face again! One of my former high school basketball teammates saw me and pretty much summed it all up "You don't know a damn thing about golf, do you?" How could you tell?

Time to Shine

Okay…so I had some work to do on my golf game. But football? Where do I start? It just so happened that the 4A state championship was coming up and one of the teams about to battle for the crown was Booker T. and Channel 8 would be broadcasting it "live." I knew the Hornets because many of them I helped coach at Carver! BTW's Head Coach, Ed Lacy, was my former head coach. The same one who guided us to the school's first title in 1967…six years earlier. I was pumped and couldn't wait to rebound from my awful showing during the golf tournament at Southern Hills.

The big crowd at Skelly Stadium, home for the University of Tulsa, was enthusiastic and anticipated a good hard-fought contest between the two best teams in the state….Booker T. Washington and Nathan Hale. I worked both sidelines in the beginning, but because of BTW's dominance, most of the game I ended up in and around its bench. Since the players and coaches knew me, my conversations with them on camera, were fluid, easy, and revealing. I was in my element and it showed. The broadcast came across as very professional, flawless. I felt bad for Nathan Hale, the Rangers didn't have a chance in this one and lost to the Hornets 39 to 7.

It would be Coach Lacy's final championship at Booker T. and solidified his remarkable legacy on the football field. During his tenure, BTW would capture state titles in 1967,'68,'69,'71 and '73. In addition to the players, Lacy received ample assistance from his coaching staff, which included Bobby Mayes, one of the best defensive minds around. He was someone I was happy to call a friend…as well as a mentor.

In addition to my weekend sportscasting duties, I was a general assignment news reporter during the week. This helped me considerably. I learned to put together "packages" or reports, from start to finish. I learned how to have a story "shot" or filmed to best illustrate what I was trying to explain…then be able to match my words to the pictures. You can write a great script but if it doesn't coordinate with your video, what good is it?

Sportscasters back then were often accused of just taking "B-roll" or action of a game, and connecting a "sound bite" or interview to it…and not have any real skills at putting together a compelling story utilizing all facets of the broadcast process. Good news reporters did it every day. I wanted to be just as good.

So, I tried to soak up as much knowledge as I could and learn from the pros around me: both in front of the camera, and behind it, at the producer's desk, operators of the studio cameras, the directors, the viewers, and so many others. No one is perfect, but I'm reaching for it…every day!

CHAPTER 6

Hangin' in Houston

LEARNING HOW TO EDIT FILM brought another stimulating test, that if I couldn't master...and I can't say I did, I needed to at least be able to communicate to an editor what I was trying to do with a particular report. This was really tough because you needed to manipulate the film's "A" roll or interview...so it coincided with certain places you wanted the "B" roll to cover, or serve as pictures for my narration.

The film would have to be developed, which in the beginning of my career could take about an hour and a half. Then you actually cut and hot spliced it into the segments you wanted to tell a story. The splicing was critical, because if not done correctly, it would come apart while it was being broadcast, and that would be the end of your day's efforts. Then the questions were being asked by the show producers, technical directors, you name it..."what happened?"

You had to be counted on to take a report from the filming of the interview, to the broadcast of the story. Many times you would be the one to "toss" it from the studio to the viewers...and need I say time was always critical and your management of it could be the difference between success and failure. All the while never wanting the folks at home see you sweat. Whew!

If you had a particularly good broadcast or report, you were smart to keep a copy and add it to your "get away" reel. It pretty much explains itself. If a job opened in another city or at another station, that reel showcased you at your very best. It was your resume, and you want to keep it updated. It didn't take me long to figure that out.

I received a chance to travel to Houston. I had never been there and figured why not? But before leaving I contacted two news directors there and inquired about possible job opportunities at their respective stations. I was pleasantly surprised when I was able to set up a couple of interviews. No agent, no head hunter, just a belief in self and the realization that if I don't try….I will never know.

I had no idea then, but John Davenport, who was at KHOU-TV Channel 11, the CBS affiliate, was one of the many reporters who interviewed us during the Black 14 incident in Laramie. I believe he was working with ABC network back then. I left the meeting with him without a concrete offer. I wasn't sure if he was serious, and I told him I had another interview in town. He wanted me to be sure I didn't make a hasty decision.

My next stop was KPRC-TV Channel 2, the NBC station. The legendary Ray Miller was Vice President of News. The instant I met Ray I knew he was a no nonsense kind of guy and yet he had a disarming smile. He wasn't a big man physically, but I would learn that he was a giant in the news business. Phil Archer, one of my soon to be co-workers, explained it this way…"To be hired by Ray Miller was like winning the lottery. He was just the best."

Once again God has put me in the right place…at the right time. There is no other way to describe or explain it. I had only been in television news eight months and I'm moving up roughly 35 markets into the top ten! As fond as I am of Tulsa, I couldn't turn this opportunity down…and the winter weather sealed it for sure. When I left Houston the sun was shining with temps in the 70's. I encountered quarter-sized, blowing snow flakes heading back to Oklahoma.

While I couldn't contain my excitement, I wasn't so carried away that I didn't realize I had a lot of work facing me. This was the big time, 5th largest city in the country, with professional sports teams to accompany it…Oilers, Astros, and Rockets. On the Collegiate scene,

The University of Houston, Rice, Houston Baptist, and Texas Southern University would keep me busy...along with all the high schools in the area. Nope, I won't be suffering from boredom...hardly.

Ray Miller was a newsman. I can't emphasize that enough. When you worked for him...you did things the right way. You could argue with him if you wanted, but in the end, he would win. Every single story that ran on Channel 2, had been inspected thoroughly by Ray, and on more than a few occasions I'm thankful they were. He was a teacher, mentor and make no mistake about it...the boss.

I learned so much from him and I wasn't the only one. Upon Ray's passing on September 27, 2008 former CBS anchorman Dan Rather was quoted as saying Miller was "so honest that you could shoot dice with him over the phone."

Syndicated columnist and man known for his opinions, Cal Thomas, said of Miller "The Pulitzer Prize would not mean as much to me as that approval from my mentor Ray Miller."

Former ABC reporter Tom Jarriel, news anchor and reporter, Paula Zahn and former U.S. Senator Kay Bailey Hutchinson are among the many journalist who felt Ray's influence and stern guidance. When Miller hired Hutchinson, she became the first female television newswoman in Texas. Longtime rival and anchorman at KTRK-TV Channel 13, Dave Ward, had this to say of Ray Miller "a true professional .He wasn't an easy man to work for. He demanded excellence and was a great news director. The Houston market was very lucky to have him."

I think you get the picture, the man was one of a kind...revered and feared. It just depended on your relationship with him. If you were one of those people he considered a bad guy, you could, and more than likely would...feel his wrath.

He was known for his journalistic intensity, black horn rim glasses, and an elegant speaking voice in his narration of the history and culture of Texas. This was very obvious during his weekly 'The Eyes of Texas' program, which Miller created and served as host from 1969 to 1999.

The Texas Association of Broadcasters designated him as a "Pioneer Broadcaster." The Texas State Legislature named him a "Texas Legend." While at Channel 2, he won a Peabody Award, the broadcast equivalent of a Pulitzer Prize. He served in both World War Two and the Korean War...and covered the Vietnam War for KPRC. He certainly had my attention, respect, and unwavering support.

REAL LIFE DRAMA...UP CLOSE AND PERSONAL

My daily duties at KPRC were pretty much similar to those at KTUL. I anchored the weekend sports, and was a general assignment reporter during the week. In addition I held down the federal building beat. That was a tough and often boring assignment. But if something "broke" it was big! The offices were basically staffed by the federal courts, CIA and Secret Service. A very "tight lipped" group who were leery and weary of outsiders. The news media were tops on that list. It took literally months to gain any acceptance and trust from those employees. About the most I could hope for was a "nugget" coming out of the clerk's office regarding a trial or case. Just a taste of something, which by itself was not worthy of broadcasting.

One incident still haunts me to this day...and, as far as my boss was concerned, was more than a morsel. A federal judge's clerk gave me some information regarding a legal issue in his court. I promised that I wouldn't report it...yet. My intent was to wait until more facts surfaced. Ray didn't see it that way. He told me, "We are in the news business!" He led our 6:00 broadcast with what I learned.

I didn't think it was worth damaging the relationships I had been cultivating. Trust was of utmost importance. Jobs were at stake if information was leaked. After our report I received a phone call from the judge's clerk. He spoke through tears and needless to say was extremely upset with me. I couldn't blame him. I felt lower than low. I don't think he lost his job, but I honestly don't know. It was a hard personal lesson learned. Protect my information and my sources...until I'm ready to reveal them!

Ray's decision to run the story that day may have been influenced by a heated ratings war that we were locked into with Channel 13, KTRK-TV. Dave Ward headed a team that included popular sportscaster Bob Allen, and consumer reporter, Marvin Zindler, who with his tinted glasses, platinum hair, and $500 dollar suits (remember this was the 70's)…had to be seen, to be believed.

He was well known for the way he signed off from his reports…" Marrrr-vin Zindler…Eyeeeeee-witness News!" He was also known for exposing unscrupulous dirty businesses, and for shutting down the "Chicken Ranch." It was the basis, among other things, for the Broadway and film musical The Best Little Whorehouse in Texas. According to news accounts, Fayette County sheriff Jim T. Flournoy physically attacked Zindler and left him with two fractured ribs. Flournoy snatched Zindler's toupee and reportedly acted as if it was a prized scalp…waving it in the air, before throwing it in the street.

May 11, 1976 started out like any other day…until, while traveling along The Southwest freeway, headed downtown from Sharpstown, we came upon a scene that was absolutely unbelievable. It's around 11 am, both sides of one of the busiest stretches of roads in the country were shut down. Debris was everywhere. It appeared, minus a crater that some kind of bomb had exploded. Cars that would normally be pushing the speed limit, were stopped in the middle of the freeway, angled in every direction imaginable. Fire trucks, ambulances, and Emergency Medical Service vehicles were everywhere.

People were running, some with kids in their arms, dust or dirt on their clothes, and expressions of horror on their blood drenched faces…scenes that were usually reserved for a Hollywood blockbuster.

But this was no movie, the nightmare was real. A tanker truck carrying 7,000 gallons of pure, undiluted industrial anhydrous ammonia, had fallen off the 610 loop, down to the freeway beneath. Anhydrous ammonia is a pungent, colorless non-flammable liquefied gas. It's used as an agricultural fertilizer and industrial refrigerant. Its fumes are suffocating. When it is released into the air, it expands rapidly, forming a large cloud that acts like a heavier-than-air gas for a period of time.

Because the vapors hug the ground initially...it causes greater danger to humans than other gases. Symptoms include eye, nose, and throat irritation. You cough up blood, have difficulty breathing, in addition to experiencing chest pain, burns, blisters, and frost bite. Exposure can be fatal at high concentrations.

Seven people died, including some who were running to escape the catastrophe, 50 to 75 yards away. Nearly 200 were injured and most of the grass and plants in the area later died. The National Transportation Safety Board would determine that the driver, traveling too fast, lost control of his rig and hit a support beam.

It didn't occur to me at the time how fortunate we were not to come along this stretch of road 15 minutes earlier. We could have been one of the victims! Instead, we went into professional mode: gathering and reporting the facts, filming this horrible scene...while helping survivors and first responders when we could.

Ray, in turn, helped us by providing mature and seasoned experience. We still had to report it on our evening newscast. The idea was to tone down our delivery and emotions...as much as possible. Not an easy thing to do when reporting on the worst accident in Houston's history.

In addition to Ray Miller, I was privileged and honored to work with some other outstanding individuals at KPRC-TV, including the aforementioned Cal Thomas, and Phil Archer, Bob Brandon, Assistant News Director Larry Weidman, anchor Larry Rasco, Carole Kneeland, weatherman Doug Johnson and his side kick Ron Stone. Thanks to them and others, Big Two News stayed "on the scene" and generally...at or near the top of the ratings.

Ron Stone, with his quick wit and engaging smile and Doug Johnson's laughter, kept the viewers in stitches and glued to the 5:00 news. Stone was called "the most popular and revered news anchor the city has ever known" according to the Houston Chronicle newspaper. Like me, Stone was another former Okie. It was said Stone was an Oklahoman by birth, and a Texan by choice. In addition to his newscasts, Ron succeeded Ray Miller as host of The Eyes of Texas in 1999. He was part of the Houston Oilers radio network. Prior to that, he broadcast Southwest Conference football games. After retiring from Channel 2 in 1992, Stone started an award winning video production firm, Stonefilms of Texas. He died of cancer May 13, 2008.

Two Country Outdoors

Bob Brandon would do things with his camera few could accomplish…as his numerous awards would attest. Following his arrival at Channel 2, he took home 30 awards in nine years and led the station through the switch from film to video tape. Bob was a two-time national Emmy Award winner. Twice he won the National Press Photographers Association top video Journalist honor, the Ernie Crisp Television Photographer of the year title, and was given the organization's highest honor when he was presented with the Joseph A. Sprague Memorial Award in 2006. In addition, Brandon was winner of the NPPA's Cliff Edom Award for his ability to inspire and motivate young photographers.

That's a lot of hardware to collect, but if you were ever fortunate enough to work with Bob you were not surprised. One of the things I enjoyed was watching and listening to him and Phil Archer swap ideas about the best approaches to—you name it…shooting photos, recording, editing.

I got the chance to spend a lot of "one on one" time with Bob during a two-year stretch. Ray put it into motion, suggesting we produce some recreational stories for the upcoming ratings period. On paper it seemed pretty cut and dry, and rather basic. Bob, however, had his own ideas and I loved them! He turned that simple suggestion by Ray into a long-running segment of our newscast. It caught our competitors flat footed…trying desperately to produce similar story lines.

One day I might be on an oil rig, out in the Gulf of Mexico, with Jacques Cousteau, during one of his memorable dives into the deep blue water. If only I had been certified in time to go down there with him! On another occasion I might be learning how to water ski, while making a complete fool of myself. Continually falling into the water…until finally I'm up on the skis and grinning like I'm posing for the latest printed version of "Believe It or Not!" Bob made it a first-class production complete with a silhouetted profile of my head and shoulders with the title, "Jay Berry's Two Country Outdoors" scrolled across the screen. It was slick!

I certainly hadn't thought of it…so I played my role of host, got out of Bob's way and let that man produce. I could be imitating Euell Gibbons, during one segment, out among the tall grass looking for edible weeds or nuts.

The Houston Livestock Show and Rodeo might be coming to town. We would ride out 50 miles or so, meet people in covered wagons, strike up a relationship, and report some of their stories. Eventually, while riding in the wagons, escort them into the area of the Astrodome where most of the participants would gather.

Last but not least, and the one I enjoyed the most…goose hunting. As usual, it was all filmed. I woke up before sunrise, kicked off the covers…thus exposing my long johns, and hopefully nothing else. I then grabbed the decoys, hunkered down in the grass, and called our feathered friends to join us. Those geese looked like 747's coming in for a landing!

We cooked a complete meal, sharing the recipes with the viewers…and ate. The evening was finished off with a homemade desert, in front of a roaring fireplace. Trust me, there was no other station in our market doing this! We worked long hours, both shooting and editing, but when we finished, we had a week's worth of unique and compelling reports. I loved it!

Luv Ya Blue!

I believe competition is that addictive connector that is found in all of us: young and old…big and tall….rich and poor…Black and White.

That urge to be the best is undeniable. If not the very best, we generally want to be better than the last time, whenever that was. It must be in our DNA, some gene that is as ubiquitous as oxygen in our blood stream. It starts innocently enough: in the household, sweeps through the neighborhood, schools, gas stations, grocery stores, churches, city hall, an entire city, surrounding towns…and beyond! Never was that more obvious than in Houston during the late 70's.

Bum Phillips is the head coach of the Oilers. He cuts a striking figure with his big trademark cowboy hat and gift of country gab that endears him to fans of the team. They know he is one of them…a hardworking, never say die competitor and a walking, talking quote machine.

"There's two kinds of coaches, them that's fired and them that's gonna be fired." "I never scrimmage Oilers against Oilers…what for? Houston isn't on our schedule." "The Dallas Cowboys may be America's team, but the Houston Oilers are Texas' team." "The harder we played the behinder we got."

Can you imagine a conversation between Bum and Yogi Berra?

Most importantly, Bum knew football and how to get the most out of his teams, although the ultimate prize, a Super Bowl title, eluded him. In 1978 he drafted Earl Campbell to help him in his quest. Earl, AKA "The Tyler Rose," grew up in Tyler, Texas, which is known for its rose bushes. Its favorite son, would soon be a thorn in the side of many NFL teams and players.

Campbell came out of the University of Texas with a bull-like body. In fact his thighs were bigger than the waist of the average person. He had legendary skills, possessing size and speed. He was a consensus All-America and winner of the coveted Heisman Trophy, symbolic of the best player in college football. Yet, I found him to be a humble, kind individual…but that changed when he was running the ball.

Many times during his career he was advised to take it easy… and not try to run over everyone in his path heading to the goal line. To which he would simply reply, in his slow and easy drawl…"I only know one way to play football." With that Campbell charged into the National Football League and displayed never before seen abilities. Earl and Bum captivated the Oilers' faithful, who were starving for the Lombardi Trophy and the undisputed title of NFL champions.

With Earl on the team, Bum had what appeared to be the final piece he needed offensively to get the job done. Dan Pastorini, a strong armed veteran at quarterback, was coming off a season in which he threw for almost 2,000 yards, but only 13 touchdowns, plus he was picked off 18 times. Surely Earl would take some of the pressure off of him. Ronnie Coleman and a young Rob Carpenter also showed promise out of the backfield. Each had rushed for 600 yards the previous year.

Big wide receiver Kenny Burrough had to be respected. He was one of the best in the league and a homerun threat thanks to his size and speed. Second year man Mike Barber, Rich Caster and Mike Renfro could give opposing defensive backs plenty to think about.

Sturdy center Carl Mauch, 6'6" left tackle Greg Sampson, a defensive end at Stanford, and right tackle Conway Hayman…anchored the offensive line, which was a mixture of youth and veterans. The fellows up front weren't the strong suit of the team, but the o-line was above average.

The defense of Curley Culp and Elvin Bethea, a couple of Pro Bowlers, along with linebacker Robert Brazile and defensive back Willie Alexander, were at the core a formidable group.

Houston would get back into the playoffs, as a Wild Card, thanks to a 10 & 6 regular season which included a four-game winning streak, including a victory on the road, against arch-rival Pittsburgh. However, there would be no home cooking in the post season. Still, the Oilers pulled off a couple of impressive wins away from the 'dome; first 17-9 in Miami, then 31-14 in New England…which sent them into the AFC Conference Championship in Pittsburgh.

The game was as ugly as the January weather for Houston fans. In a freezing rain, Campbell couldn't find any footing or place to run. The Oilers turned the ball over nine times, including five interceptions by

Pastorini. The Steel Curtain was as good as advertised in a 34-5 victory over the Oilers.

Pittsburgh would hold off Dallas 35-31 in the Super bowl, while the Oilers were left to think about what could have been. They found a bonafide diesel in Campbell, who showed all of his skills during a Monday night thriller against Miami. He would get the corner, go around right end…and travel 81 yards for a touchdown in a 35-30 victory for Houston. Big Earl would end the night with 199 yards rushing, finishing the season with 1,450…tops in the league. He also added 13 touchdowns.

Bum Phillips didn't win his title, but the city wasn't about to go quietly. In fact, the party was just getting started in Houston…as pom-pom waving fans were worked into a frenzy, and let the team know…' Luv Ya Blue!' Soon the NFL wouldn't have to wonder what that meant.

The pompoms actually appeared the previous season during that dramatic Monday night win over Miami. Now, they were must haves for fans who were also waiving 'Luv Ya Blue' signs, painting their faces, holding pep rallies, and singing to the tops of their lungs…

> "Look out football, here we come,
> Houston Oilers number one. Houston has the Oilers, the greatest football team.
> We take the ball from goal to goal like no one's ever seen.
> We're in the air, we're on the ground…always in control
> and when you say Oilers, you're talking Super Bowl!"

Singer/Songwriter Mark Hayes wrote and recorded the song after the Oilers ended last season, in disappointing fashion. Now, it's become a rallying cry for the faithful and a sure-fire way to pump up everyone in blue! Super Bowl? Nothing else will do!

Sadly, another outstanding season would end abruptly in Pittsburgh, a game shy of the intended goal. The Steelers were AFC champs again thanks to a 27-13 victory…and in part by a blown call by the officials, that wiped out…with the extra point, a tying Mike Renfro touchdown in the 3rd quarter.

The team would be greeted by a jam-packed Astrodome...and Bum Phillips would issue his famous statement....

"One year ago we knocked on the door! This year we beat on it! Next year we're going to kick the son of a bitch in!"

All Good Things Must...

In 1980, Bum and his boys gave it another valiant attempt, even put together another 11 & 5 season. But that door they were hoping to kick in? They didn't come close, losing to the Oakland Raiders 27 to 7 in a Wild Card showdown. In an interesting twist, Oilers owner, Bud Adams traded for Ken Stabler and sent Pastrorini to Oakland. He didn't get to play against his old team in the playoffs, after breaking his leg. Jim Plunkett stepped in at quarterback and guided the Raiders through the post season, culminating with a Super Bowl victory over Philadelphia.

Bum would also leave after the 1980 season, having been fired by Adams three days following the loss to Oakland. He would head East...down I-10 and become head coach of the New Orleans Saints. Earl Campbell would join his former coach in 1984...via a trade six games into the season. Big Earl would retire after the 1985 campaign, having established himself as one of the greatest running backs to ever play football...college or pro. Campbell was inducted into the College Football Hall of Fame in 1990. A year later he went into the Pro Football Hall of Fame.

He paid a price playing the game he loves. He has been diagnosed with arthritis and spinal stenosis, leaving him with constant pain and muscle weakness. Because of his difficulty walking, he uses a cane or walker and for longer distances a wheelchair. It's difficult to see him this way, but I'm reminded of his statement when he entered the NFL..." I only know one way to play this game."

1979 would be my last year in Houston. It wasn't something I planned, but as it was when I left Tulsa...an opportunity I couldn't pass up. Chicago came calling and I had to listen. It was a crazy time for me, having purchased my first home in the Southwest part of the city. In fact, my new drapes arrived when I was headed out the door.

This new opportunity included not only increased pay: but more vacation time and the ability to be a full time sportscaster, with a Monday thru Friday, 5:00 time slot. I also would be expected to generate reports for our late 10:00 news. Plus the new station, WLS-TV, was owned and operated by ABC. There was prestige in that, and we're talking the number three market in the country.

Still, leaving Houston was hard! People had welcomed me into their homes and shown me the best five years of my life. So many memories, so many good times, plus my co-workers would be missed. Ray Miller and I tried to come up with a competitive contract to match WLS. In fact, I declined its first offer. But in the end, I just couldn't turn down the opportunity. In addition, I must admit, I wanted to see where I was in my career and if I could be successful in Chicago. I felt I could compete…and hold my own anywhere. So Channel 7, here I come, but not without memories from one of the greatest cities in the world.

I was just eight months into television news when I arrived from Tulsa. Now I'm leaving with awards from United Press International and Associated Press as the top Sports Broadcaster in Texas for 1977. Frankly, I was never into trying to pick up awards, it was a personal thing. I wanted, and expected my very best every day. When it was over, let the chips fall where they may. Anything I received in the way of plaques during my career, someone else put my name into the competition. So let me give thanks to the writers, producers, archivists and directors who did enter the competitions, because were it not for you…I would be "plaque-less."

Rudy T. Could've Died

I also want to thank The Houston Rockets for some thrilling basketball action as they climbed that highly competitive NBA ladder. Playing at Hofheinz Pavilion, on the University of Houston campus, the team showed promise while winning half its games during the 1974-75 season. Led by Rudy "T" Tomjanovich (the former University of Michigan standout), little "C" Calvin Murphy, and Mike Newlin, the rockets had fire power...but their journey was just getting started.

They lost some ground the next season, and head coach Johnny Egan was replaced by Tom Nissalke. I liked Nissalke who was very business-like on the court, yet still approachable. The fans took a liking to him as well, when the team finished first in the Central Division after adding Moses Malone, in a trade with Buffalo, and guard John Lucas out of the University of Maryland. Lucas, who was the first overall selection in the NBA draft, was also an All-America tennis player and would play both sports as a pro.

That 1976-77 team was a nightmare for opposing defenses! Rudy T had averages of 21.6 points and 8.4 rebounds, little C threw in 17.9 points per game, Moses delivered 13.5 points and 13.1 rebounds, guard Mike Newlin added 12.7 points, and Lucas chipped in 11.1 points and 5.6 assists. Yet, with all that fire power the Rockets would fall to Doctor J, Julius Erving and the Philadelphia 76ers...four games to two, in the Eastern Conference finals. Better luck next year? There are no guarantees, in life...and certainly not sports.

That was never more evident than in the 1977-78 season. The year was just getting started. It's December, and the Rockets' Kevin Kunnert gets into a fight with Kermit Washington of the Los Angeles Lakers. Rudy T innocently rushes down from the other end of the court, looking to be a peacemaker. These are big men going at it. Washington is a powerfully built man, 6'8" 230. Kunnert is 7-feet and weighs 230... and Rudy T is 6'8" and 220.

Kareem Abdul Jabbar is holding Kunnert, who is doubled over. Jabbar pushes Washington away. Tomjanovich, the Rockets' captain, continues advancing towards Washington, who thinks Tomjanovich is going to join in the fight. That was never his intent. Washington delivers one of the most devastating punches ever thrown, in or out of the ring and catches the defenseless Tomjanovich square in the face. Some have likened it to being thrown from a car going 50 miles per hour.

The damage to Tomjanovich's face is extensive…it nearly killed him. The all-star forward suffered a concussion, leakage of spinal fluid into the brain cavity, and fractures of the skull, jaw, and nose. Washington is suspended without pay for 60 days and fined $10,000. "My face was kind of hanging there," says Tomjanovich. "If you could have seen me, you'd know I was a human being, but I looked like a monster." He would spend two weeks in the hospital, with towels over the mirror in his room to hide his broken-up face…from himself, but he would return next season.

In addition to what happened to Tomjanovich, Moses Malone missed 23 games because of an injury. The Rockets finished the year sixth in the Central Division with a 28-64 record. Tomjanovich, still suffering effects from being punched by Kermit Washington, returned to action in 1978-79 and eventually picked up where he left off, scoring an average of 19 points a game. A healthy Moses Malone became a force and was named Most Valuable Player in the league with numbers indicative of his status…24.8 points and a league leading 17. 6 rebounds. Calvin Murphy increased his production by throwing in over 20 points a game. The Rockets would finish second in the Central, but were bounced out of the playoffs in the first round by the Atlanta Hawks, who were led by John Drew, Eddie Johnson and Dan Roundfield.

On the diamond the Astros, with the likes of: Bob Watson, Cliff Johnson, Cesar Cedeno, Enos Cabell, Joe Nikero, Jose Cruz, Greg Gross and by all means J.R. Richard…kept it interesting. All J.R. had to do was toss his glove on the field and the best competitors would wilt. At 6'8" and coming off that mound…he was very imposing, then add his 100 mile per hour fast ball. Believe me, you didn't want to dig in at the batter's box! The wins were hard to come for the Astros, but in those days, they appeared to be giving all they had.

Mr. Hockey and the Aeros

Meanwhile, over at the Sam Houston Coliseum, and then the Summit, I was learning a whole new game…hockey. What better teacher than

Mr. Hockey himself, Gordie Howe, with sons Mark and Marty! The Howe's may have had the most recognizable names on the Houston Aeros, but they had plenty of help. Head Coach Bill Dineen, Poul Popiel, Larry Lund, Ron Grahame, John Tonelli, Rich Preston, and Terry Ruskowski turned the Aeros into one of the most successful... and thus popular franchises in the World Hockey Association. I liked Ruskowski a lot. He was a little pit bull on the ice, ready to take on all challengers.

Houston would win four consecutive AVCO CUPS, the WHA's answer to the NHL's version of the Stanley Cup...if I might put it that way. Despite the Aeros success, they were left out when the two leagues finally decided to merge. The Aeros would fold in the summer of '78. When Mark retired as a member of the Detroit Red Wings, Gordie's former team, he was the last member of the Aeros to be playing in the National Hockey League.

HOUSTON MEET MR. MONTANA

The Houston Cougars enjoyed quite a bit of success under Head Coach Bill Yeoman, during my stay in the Lone Star state. But they learned a tough lesson in the '79 Cotton Bowl game, and a little something about a fellow named Joe Montana.

Houston had its fans literally partying in the stands. The players on the bench joined them when the Cougars went up 20-12 at the half, thus erasing a 12-point deficit. Houston would add two more touchdowns and lead it 34-12 with 7:37 left in the contest. Montana, suffering from the chills...stayed in the locker room as late as he could during half-time. But he finally emerged to bring Notre Dame all the way back, in one of the most exciting finishes I have ever witnessed. With two seconds left in the game, and having put down some chicken soup during intermission, Montana, on what turns out to be the last play of the game...hits Kris Haines in the corner of the end zone. With the extra point, the Cougars are laid to rest 35-34! The Irish are still talking about that one...maybe the Cougars too.

The Pony Express

In the Prep ranks, a couple of running backs were making names for themselves. Over at Stratford High School, Jesse Craig James set the 4A single-season rushing record with 2,411 yards in 15 games…and was offered a contract to play baseball for the New York Yankees.

52 miles west, down the Katy freeway, Eric Demetri Dickerson was setting his own records for Class AA Sealy high school by rushing for 2,642 yards and 37 touchdowns. He also was a state champion in track, clocking a 9.4 in the 100- yard dash. The dynamic duo would form the "Pony Express" at Southern Methodist University. They both were extremely successful for the Mustangs, but allegations of recruiting improprieties, such as a rumored new Pontiac Trans Am for Dickerson, plagued the SMU football program. It would be placed on probation in 1981, resulting in a television and bowl ban the following season. The ten violations listed in the NCAA report didn't include purchase of a car. Dickerson produced paperwork that said his grandmother bought him the automobile.

Trivia time: The Houston Astros' home field was the Astrodome. It was built, among other reasons, to insure no home games would be cancelled because of rain. Yet that is exactly what happened June 15, 1976. The only rainout in Astrodome history.

Remember? Flooding prevented fans, umpires, and other stadium personnel from entering the stadium.

CHAPTER 7

State Street...That Great Street

I KNOW IT'S REDUNDANT, BUT change does bring changes, especially when you have to move....everything. However, I believed Chicago was worth it...as were the opportunities and challenges it presented. Just as was the case in Houston, I negotiated the contract myself. Other potential employees might feel decidedly different about this, and they could be right. But, after gathering as much information I could, and with a little more of this, and a little more of that...which included turning down the original offer, I accepted the deal.

I had more than doubled the salary I earned in Houston, added two more weeks of vacation, and moved from weekends...to a Monday thru Friday slot. I was asked to provide extra help initially, by anchoring one of the weekend days. I had been assured by Johnny Mies, my news director and the one I negotiated my contract, that he had been in his position for ten years. He told me WLS-TV had been a solid number one during his tenure, and he wasn't going anywhere.

The new schedule was challenging. Getting used to the way things operated added to that. But, hard work wasn't anything I shied away from, so I'm focused on what I need to do and anticipating when things would slow down.

My contract gave me a month to find a place to live free of charge. Until then, my temporary home was the Hyatt Regency on Wacker, a few blocks from WLS, which was located at State and Lake. I didn't get to see very much of The Hyatt, I was too busy working...often 12 hour days. So house hunting was difficult, with basically only one day a week to shop. In addition, Chicago covers a lot of land. I quickly learned what you can rent or buy in Houston can be a lot more expensive in the Windy City. Doubling my salary was good…but I'm thinking having a little more money would have helped. Isn't that usually the case?

I would never consider buying a home in a brand new market, not until I felt secure enough to do it. I signed a three year contract, but the station still had "out" clauses, in which after a period of time it could terminate the deal. Not so for the vast majority of "on-camera" employees. This actually was pretty standard; and the deal I received was better than many…an 18 month window for the station. Some employees were under a 90-day "out" period, if they had a contract at all! Welcome to television in the big time.

So I wanted a 12- month rental, then I would assess the situation. That perfect "spot" was proving to be pretty elusive. Also to consider in this equation: how far will I have to commute? Will I take the El, bus, or what? Drive? I would have to think about the cost of parking. Decisions, decisions.

Johnny Mies, loved, and I mean absolutely loved Chicago. He didn't pronounce it Shee-CAH-go…but ShA-CAW-go. I couldn't blame him for the fondness he had for his hometown, even though I bet he would have easily moonlighted at the visitors' bureau for a minimum fee. The city is gorgeous: The Chicago River, Lake Michigan? The ever changing skyline? Grant Park? Navy Pier? Michigan Avenue? The place has a lot to be proud of, and these Chicagoans, like Houstonians, believe in expressing it.

My number one choice for an apartment is within a ten minute walking distance from the station. How sweet would that be? But no vacancies, or so I have been told. However, a return visit, and another enquiry proves nothing could be further from the truth. In fact, there are units that have never been occupied! It's a different individual in the apartment office today, and this one is apparently in a relationship with an African-American, unlike the previous person. I am floored! Its 1979…not 1959 or 1969! I thought by now, the only color that mattered, especially here in this world class city…was green, as in the color of money! Well, apparently not. I like the one on the 47th floor, overlooking the lake to the south. You can sign me up and with the quickness….thank you.

Some of my co-workers predicted that I would be selling one of my two cars. They were right. My building had below ground parking, but that wasn't free, plus a car needs to be insured….good thing I could walk to work, which turned out to be huge. In Houston a car is just as necessary as air conditioning.

Speaking of needs, I could use a reliable barber. To the average person that may not seem to be a big deal, but I work inside that box that sits in your home or apartment. Everyone gets to see what you look like. Bad hair days are not acceptable, if you can prevent them. In Richard Gordon I had a reliable one in Houston. He used a perm to relax my hair. He then would "blow it out" so it had a nice roundness about it. Think of my afro as a full moon. When I went to my first barber in Chicago, one who claimed he knew how to handle chemicals, I felt one side of my hair looked more like a crescent moon.

Regardless of how I tried to "angle" my body on the studio set, I still felt self-conscious. Third biggest television market in the country, potentially millions of viewers watching, and I am not looking my best….not even close! Another new barber thought a different "do" would be the best way to hide my imperfections. He was right, but it came with its own issues. It was called a Jheri curl. You still had to perm your hair, but watch out…too much activator and it will become a "scary" curl. More on that later, but for now my hope is that my "crescent moon look" had been eclipsed for good!

Inside of Channel 7 are people who helped WLS-TV become a force in Chicago television. People like the legendary, bow tie wearing Fahey Flynn, Joel Daly, John Drury, Tim Weigel, Terry Murphy, Jay Levine, Frank Mathie, Rob Weller and newcomers Diane Allen, Larry

Moore, Mary Ann Childers, Joan Esposito, Jim Avila, Chuck Goudie, Russ Ewing, Jim Ramsey, and Jack Jones, among a host of others... including Bob Petty, Rosemarie Gulley, Editorial Director Bill Campbell, and my countless co-workers behind the cameras.

Tim Weigel, a Yale graduate, was a Chicago legend in the making. He was known for his writing ability, quick wit and daredevil style; while handing out his Weigel Wieners to those he deemed deserving of his blooper awards. Tim was the sports director when I arrived. I believe Johnny Mies thought, because of my Two Country Outdoors segments in Houston, we would play off each other...as he sought new blood and diversity for his news team. We never talked about it, but it's a feeling I had. Tim was playing minor league football at this time and called himself "White Shoes Weigel." The hitting was real... as was his gear, all the way down to those white shoes! But jelling with Tim was not in the cards. Much too fast paced in Chicago to duplicate what I did in Houston, not enough time. But we shared a lot of laughs and our experiences in the world of sports.

DE PAUL'S DEMONS

Upon my arrival to this city known for its broad shoulders, I found it rather ironic that when it came to sports...Chicago's hope for success rested on the back of little DePaul University. Small in size only, because in college basketball you couldn't get much bigger. Led by its aw shucks, gapped tooth, lovable Coach Ray Meyer...the Blue Demons were making NCAA appearances seem as common as skyscrapers in the Loop. But each year they left their faithful and the entire city of Chicago for that matter, wondering...what's going on?

During a seven year stretch...from 1977 thru 1984, DePaul never won less than 21 games. Four times the NCAA Tournament made it a No.1 seed...and once, No. 2. Yet, the Blue Demons only have seven wins to show for their efforts...including a third place finish in 1978-79, when they picked up four of their tournament victories. Three times as a No.1 seed, they were upset in the opening game. Making those numbers even more of a head-scratcher, was the talent on those teams. No less than five future NBA draft choices were on each of those squads, topped by a mind-boggling nine on the 1982-83 team that finished runner-up in the National Invitational Tournament.

Mark Aguirre, a prolific scoring machine, out of Westinghouse High School in Chicago, was the biggest name among the DePaul notables drafted into the National Basketball Association. He was 6'6" and his size, shooting touch, and skills enabled him to score from anywhere on the court…from three-point range to rim-rattling dunks, he was a handful for defenders.

Aguirre averaged over 25 points a game as a freshman, 26.8 and 23.0 during his sophomore and junior seasons. Before his career ended, he was honored by numerous organizations as College Basketball's Player of the Year. He also was a two time All-America. But the thing Aguirre wanted most, an NCAA championship trophy, proved elusive. He and the Blues Demons came close during the Final Four in 1979…before falling to Larry Bird and Indiana State, 76 to 74. Since Aguirre was the most visible and best player, the disappointment of the fans and media was often directed at him. It became personal at times.

I didn't understand that, and felt it was extremely unfair. Aguirre was in college, not a professional. Even if he were, he was still human, with feelings. This I believe, led to his swagger at times. He could appear combative. Probably the man who best understood what Aguirre was dealing with, was his coach Ray Meyer.

Meyer had been chasing a national championship since 1942 and would finish his career with 37 winning seasons and 724 victories. He was called simply "coach" by those who knew him, however they realized Meyer's sometimes easy going demeanor hid what he really was…a fierce competitor! Those tournament losses cut deep. His players knew to take a wide berth during and after some of those disappointing upsets. Meyer retired following the 1983-84 season after, as the No.1 seed in the Midwest, he and DePaul were upset by Wake Forest 73-71 in the Sweet 16. Meyer's son and former player, Joey, would become DePaul's new coach. Ray Meyer passed away March 17, 2006. He was 92.

Mark Aguirre would leave DePaul after his junior year. In 1981, Dallas made him the number one selection in the NBA draft. Aguirre continued to produce big numbers offensively after turning pro...averaging over 24 points a game with the Mavericks, including a career best 29.5 in 1983-84. But in order to finally get a championship, he would have to change his game...and he did.

THE STING

Professionally speaking, the Chicago Sting gave those of us in the media and fans plenty to talk about; providing excitement and city pride during my time in Chicago. The team was a dream come true for Chicago's own Lee Stern. He was a leading commodities broker, who in 1974 took an expensive gamble that his hometown would accept soccer as a major league sport. From a modest beginning of only 4,500 fans at the first home game, the Sting would eventually entertain 40,000 at Comiskey Park...and a record crowd of over 58,000 in Montreal's Olympic Stadium.

Through trial and error Stern found his coach, in Willy Roy, who had migrated with his family from Germany...and settled in Chicago. Roy, a former all-star player himself, knew the kind of roster he needed to successfully compete in the North American Soccer League. By 1981 Roy had the roster he craved, thanks in part to some signees by former Coach Malcolm Musgrove.

A trio of strikers and future Hall of Famers; Karl-Heinz Granitza, Arno Steffenhagen, and Pato Margetic supplied most of the offense, Frantz Mathieu some glue-like defense and with reliable Phil Parkes and Dieter Ferner shining in goal...the Sting were ready to roll and deliver Chicago a long awaited title.

It's hard for me to believe, that Chicagoans had not celebrated a major sports title since the '63 Bears. But as was proven by the Houston Oilers, these things don't come easy. Like the Bears, the Sting's title would have to be earned against another New York team, the explosive Cosmos and its mega-star Giorgio Chinaglia. Toronto was the setting and Soccer Bowl '81 (the NASL's equivalent of the Super Bowl) the occasion.

The two teams knew each other very well and plenty of offense was expected. But the script was flipped. Goose eggs were showing on the scoreboard after 90 minutes, prompting some smart mouth reporter to broadcast..."There is nothing more boring than a scoreless soccer game." I couldn't have been more wrong! Because as the sudden death overtime approached, also came the realization that the agony of losing this thing would be devastating, should the Sting come up short. Each opportunity, each rush, each kick could be it… bring on the cheers or tears.

Pato Margetic was oh so close in the extended period, but no! Ingo Peter hits the crossbar, and then the upright with a header…man! Chinaglia, the NASL's all-time leading scorer, sends one just wide of Parkes…whew! Frantz Mathieu, in particular, has him covered like a blanket, unnnn-beeee-lievable!

Overtime failed to settle the issue…on to the shootout, with 37,000 fans, including 6,000 from Chicago, gasping with every play. Karl-Heinz Granitza once again comes through in a starring role, tying it at four…with one round left. Stings' goalie Dieter Ferner comes up with a great save, setting the stage for Rudy Glenn. The former Indiana star gets it to trickle past Cosmos goalie Hubert Birkenmeier, leaving just one more successful defense standing in the way of the NASL Championship. Toronto's own Bob Irausci has his attempt swallowed up by Dieter Ferner and the Sting win it…1-nothing, as the jubilant crowd rushes the field! Chicago has its championship, but who would have thought it would be delivered by an upstart soccer team and not the usually heavy favored DePaul basketball team. Go figure!

They Called him...Sweetness!

Over at Soldier field, I encounter an incredible competitor with an unusual name for a football player..."Sweetness." That was the nickname for number 34, Walter Payton. The Bears running back was very different from the "Tyler Rose." Payton used all kinds of styles to get his extra yards. He would try and run over you, if necessary, but he also had a "stutter-step," a high kick and change of speed if you will. He also had quickness in his arsenal. If all else failed and he was close enough to the goal line or the first down marker, he would contort his body and turn into a gymnast...vaulting or leaping over would-be tacklers. You would never know what he would try, which kept defenders on their heels, not wanting to become another highlight for "Sweetness." He would rush for at least 1200 yards in ten of his 13 seasons in the NFL, while setting numerous records on his way to the Pro Football Hall of Fame.

A 10-6 record in 1979, and a first round loss in the wild card game against Philadelphia, was the best "Da Bears" would do during my stay in the Windy City. It turned out to be the only winning season for Head Coach Neil Armstrong, who was fired after a 6-10 record in 1981. The Bears simply needed more help for Payton. On the field and off he kept things light, until game time. He was a jokester and everyone was fair game...even me. My Jheri curl was usually his target. Payton would start on me before I could even make it to the practice field. He was relentless, same as he was during games. Guess who was sporting a Jheri curl the next season? Yep...Sweetness!

There are special people in our lives we are fortunate to encounter, usually when we least expect it. Walter Payton is that example for me...as he was for practically everyone who met him. No matter how many numbers or statistics you attribute to him...they don't even come close to describing who he was and how he should be remembered. Walter Payton passed away November 1, 1999. Roughly ten months prior to his death he revealed he had a rare liver disease which may have led to bile duct cancer. He was 45.

ROCKET RICHARD AND THE BLACKHAWKS

My first visit to old Chicago Stadium was to watch the Black Hawks practice, and to my surprise, on the ice were Terry Ruskowski and Rich Preston…a couple of former Houston Aeros. It almost felt like old home week…for a day. Terry was a favorite, because even though he was listed at 5'9" and 168 pounds, he had a heart as big as Mount Rushmore. Terry or "Roscow" as he was called, would fight anyone while taking up for his teammates. It was a big reason he became the only player in major professional hockey to serve as captain on four teams…Houston Aeros, Chicago Blackhawks, Los Angeles Kings, and Pittsburgh Penguins.

Rich Preston joined the Black Hawks after picking up MVP honors during the 1979 World Hockey Association (WHA) playoffs with the Winnipeg Jets. I remember him as a cerebral type player and wasn't surprised, when after retirement, Rich became a coach.

The two WHA standouts joined a team in Chicago that had its challenges but also consecutive first place finishes in the Smythe Division. The 1979-80 playoffs produced a series elimination of St. Louis and ended the Black Hawks' 16 game losing streak in the post season.

My hockey knowledge received a huge boost covering the Aeros in Houston. But I learned I still had a long way to go, thanks to a mispronunciation on an evening telecast. It happened to involve one of the all-time greats in the National Hockey League. Maurice "Rocket" Richard is what the copy read, regarding the Hall of Fame right wing of The Montreal Canadiens. The phones in the sports office lit up like a Christmas tree, with angry fans ready to call me every unimaginable name in their vocabulary. Richard in French, as everyone knows BUT me (since I never took French) is pronounced Reeecharrrdah, rolling the second set of r's!

Richard is like a hockey God, who played for one of the original six teams of the National Hockey League (Montreal Canadiens, Chicago Black Hawks, Detroit Red Wings, New York Rangers, Boston Bruins, and Toronto Maple Leafs) and I had just dishonored him and desecrated his name, according to the irate callers!

No place to run...no place to hide. It's one of those embarrassing moments that even my wife won't let me live down, readily willing to share my gaffe with others! That's live broadcasting folks. Once it's released...that's it, you can't take it back.

I'm reminded of the national broadcasts of the 2014 Oscars when John Travolta mispronounces Idina Menzel's name, Steve Harvey awarding the Miss Universe title to the wrong contestant in 2015, Warren Beatty and Faye Dunaway at the 2017 Oscars, incorrectly announcing "La La Land" as the Best Picture instead of "Moonlight," the actual winner, and Fergie's performance of The National Anthem, at the National Basketball Association's 2018 All-Star game. I feel their pain...big time!

A City Divided

Spend any length of time in Chicago and you quickly realize it is a divided city. Northside vs. Southside or the other way around, if you prefer. For natives there are no options, you are either one or the other. The differences can range from the neighborhoods, to the restaurants, and certainly the baseball teams.

But in the late 70's and early 80's, neither the Cubs nor the White Sox had anything to brag about. I guess Cubs fans might say, at least we didn't stoop to "Disco Demolition Night." It was another promotion to put people in the seats and it did, though their intentions didn't have much to do with baseball. 20,000 were expected, but an estimated 50,000 showed up at Comiskey to see exploding disco records. This was during a doubleheader between Detroit and Chicago. The first game was played without incident. But in between the two contests, the playing field was damaged, both by the explosions and rowdy fans. The White Sox were forced to forfeit the second game.

It's been speculated that this event helped kill disco much to the delight of hard core rockers. That has been debated, but White Sox pitcher Rich Wortham, a Texan, said he knew one thing for sure "This wouldn't have happened if they had country and western night."

The Chicago Bulls, much like the Cubs and Sox, suffered during the end of the 70's and beginning of the 80's. They made the playoffs in 80-81 and knocked off the New York Knicks before being swept by the Boston Celtics.

There wouldn't be another winning season for eight years…four years after the arrival of Michael Jordan and those memorable battles with the Bad Boys of Detroit. I would have a front row seat.

CHAPTER 8

Motown - My Kind of Town

WITHIN A MONTH OF MY arrival in Chicago, Johnny Mies...who had been News Director for ten years, was gone. He was the one I negotiated my contract with and the one I made an agreement to work at least one weekend day until the fall, about six months. I definitely had concerns regarding my future and wanted off that six day work schedule.

Channel 7 continued to promote me in the newspapers, with advertising that also featured other members of our staff. One of my recipes was even spotlighted in the Chicago Sun Times newspaper: Groundnut Stew with peanut sauce served over brown rice...garnished with pineapples, scallions, and peanuts, thank you very much.

During an interview with the Chicago Defender, a weekly African-American newspaper, I learned from reporter Raymond Richardson... that I was the first Black sportscaster to work at WLS-TV. My third job in the television industry and the third time I'm the first...or the only African-American in a so-called prime time position. I didn't think a lot about it, except inwardly I put more pressure on myself to be the very best. I wanted to show that Black people had the capability of being successful on television and hopefully open doors for others. I was well aware of the sacrifices by so many before me, who indirectly put me in this position. So, the thought of me being a trailblazer never once entered my mind.

When I think of people who feel I am being given something, they should also realize I must achieve to stay in my positions. It wasn't announced or broadcast that the industry was trying to become reflective of its viewers; and it wasn't like there was a collective pool of experienced personnel to choose from. I believe the powers at the stations, across the nation, were courageous, smart, and sensitive in their pursuit to level the playing field, and should have been applauded for their efforts.

I would soon be joined by Jack Jones at Channel 7. He had formerly worked in Philadelphia and was an African-American as well. Jack was one of the news anchors. He had a smooth, polished delivery and a conversational manner. I thought if anyone was going to make it into a permanent Monday thru Friday position, it would be him. The weekday jobs offered more money, so it wasn't just an ego trip.

But the two of us worked weekends exclusively. Eventually that became an issue for some viewers, who thought we should have one of the better, higher profiled positions. It was not something I promoted, but I would certainly accept any help I could get.

When the next news director took over, he made it clear that he did not negotiate with me. The language and terms I verbally agreed to with Johnny Mies did not relate to him. So the weekends would become permanent and I would report during the week. I would not have left Houston for this assignment and I wasn't happy. The good news was the salary I negotiated remained the same, I no longer had to work six days a week, and I still had a job. That wasn't the case for some of my colleagues at the station. They were job hunting thanks to a couple of "shake ups" at the station.

When the end of my contract approached, I had a meeting with the general manager. He told me I could remain in my present position as long as I wanted, but I wouldn't advance into a Monday thru Friday slot. Decision time, I could decide to try and wait him out because people in his position didn't hang around forever, or I could shake his hand and thank him for being direct and honest. I chose the latter. I immediately started looking for an agent and another opportunity, even though I had three months left on my contract. I am 29 and not ready to settle. I've worked Tulsa, Houston and now Chicago. I am still standing. Time to find out what's next, and with confidence that...I can do this!

One of the biggest sports agents in the country happened to be a neighbor of mine. I told him about my situation, hoping he would represent me. Unfortunately he only handled athletes, but steered me to his partner, who concentrated on talent in the media. I was told not to worry about anything. He would contact his partner, who would begin immediately to secure me another position.

You ever have one of those sales people who says you're gonna love it, without having a clue about what you love? A few months pass and I'm told by the agent who handles on-camera personnel, there have been conversations with stations in other parts of the country, however he was still looking around. "Don't worry...I will take care of this, enjoy the summer "...I'm told. A few months later he calls and basically throws up his hands saying, "I can't do anything for you."

I get a bill for $18. I can't believe it! Don't get me wrong, I'm thankful it wasn't a larger bill, but you can hardly send postage for that amount! I ask, what about Detroit? He says it's no longer on the table. I was bummed and my head was spinning, again. Now What? How about another opportunity for God to show up and show out. I got a call the very next day from an agent. What market are you calling about I ask? He said...Detroit.

It's a crisp autumn afternoon with temps in the 60's. There is the first hint of the trees turning colors. The sun streaming through them helps paint a perfect picture of early fall. I have been sitting at this spot too long, just drifting in my rented 16-foot aluminum fishing boat... that's powered by a 40 horse Johnson/ Evinrude. Not too big...not too small, just right for Pine Lake. I've got my radio set on WJLB, and at the moment, The Whispers are singing my song…"And the Beat Goes On." How appropriate!

When word leaked that I was headed to Detroit, the comments were usually the same… "Detroit? Why are you going there?" "You mean you're leaving Chicago for Detroit?", "Are you serious or delirious?" I must admit my first and only trip to Detroit didn't leave me with the best impression, but it had little to do with the area. I was in town to report on Super Bowl 16, featuring San Francisco against Cincinnati at the Pontiac Silverdome.

It was the first time that this event was held in a cold-weather city, and as far as I was concerned…it could be the last. The January snow was deep. It was cold…real cold. To make matters worse we were being shuttled between Dearborn and Pontiac…or Troy; to get any information we could from the coaches, players, or the NFL for that matter. On a good day that's a 40 minute trip…during those Super Bowl preparations it easily took twice as long, which made for many logistical headaches, trying to cover both teams while filing reports for the daily newscasts.

But today, I'm gazing through water that has a touch of green to it. I can see down at least 15 – 20 feet…with my polarized sun glasses, maybe even further. Surprisingly, Pine Lake, which is one of a cluster of lakes in West Bloomfield, has an abundance of nice size fish, in many varieties. The deepest part is 90 feet. I am surrounded by homes with beautifully manicured lawns and incredible views of the water. Yet, I am only 15 minutes from work and my own home.

This is what doesn't come into the discussion when people make disparaging remarks about Detroit. In my opinion it is one of the best kept secrets in our great country. Granted…West Bloomfield, Southfield, Royal Oak, Rochester Hills, and Farmington Hills among others, are suburbs. But today I could have been on the Detroit River, which connects to Lake St. Clair and offers panoramic views of both downtown Detroit and Windsor, Canada.

Does Detroit have its share of problems? Absolutely! But name a major city in the United States that doesn't…and as I'm writing this,

Detroit is enjoying an amazing revitalization. I have been blessed to work and live in some unique cities, each with its own individual strengths and weaknesses. I can honestly tell you Detroit and its surrounding areas don't take a back seat to any of them.

Other pluses for me? I'm still working for one of the ABC owned and operated stations…WXYZ-TV. I am doing the sports at 6:00, Monday thru Friday. My money for the first year won't change from what I was making in Chicago, but will increase each year the following three years. I don't have to tell you the cost of living between Chicago and Detroit allowed for me to basically enjoy a significant increase. It was a good contract. Did I actually get everything that it said I would? No. But that's the nature of this business…give and take (while you can). Bottom line for me? It turns out to be a 23-year position, supplying memories I never could have imagined.

THE BLACK 14 REVISTED

My employment at Channel Seven in Detroit, brought back some previously explored topics. Once again I learned I was a first. First Black sportscaster at WXYZ. By now I am pretty used to it…comes with the territory.

But what I didn't expect appeared in bold print. "Jay Berry's odyssey: Black 14 to Ch. 7." That was my introduction to Detroit, courtesy of a Free Press headline and interview. I was conflicted, because why not mention my successes during a ten year career that included being named by the Associated Press as the Best Sportscaster in Texas? I felt The Black 14 incident had a negative connotation to it and yet, as I pointed out in the interview, I know we didn't do anything wrong. When you can't ask your coach a question without being kicked off the team, that is wrong! I just wanted the public to be able to judge me for the work I produce and I am thankful it gave me the opportunity.

Another newspaper article not only brought up the Black 14 incident, but also included my hair…right down to my Jheri curl perm! It left me shaking my head and I will admit, laughing a little. My hair was longer than I wanted it to be, but I was shell shocked after my first experience with a barber in Chicago. I hadn't found one in Detroit. So my curls were pretty evident.

Bill Bonds...the Sun King

Something else that was clear, Channel 7 had a very strong following in metro Detroit. It was a definite number one, thanks in part to a behind the scenes and on-camera staff that included among countless others: John Kelly and Marilyn Turner, Diana Lewis, Doris Biscoe, Rich Fisher, Jac LeGoff, Erik Smith, Dayna Eubanks, Rob Kress, and Jerry Hodak. But Bill Bonds was the main anchor and the main man. If you didn't know that, he would let you know it...and he wouldn't be bashful about it!

Bonds was the most popular figure on Detroit television, yet also the most polarizing at the same time. He was the fourth pip in Gladys Knight's singing group, the smartest in the room...including the living rooms he was welcomed into...and others he invaded.

Bonds was clever and smart, with a flair for the dramatic. With eyebrow arched and toupee tightly positioned...and sometimes not, Bonds was must see TV before it became a catch phrase. One night he might be challenging Detroit Mayor Coleman A. Young to a fistfight, with the money going to charity...or he has United States Senator Orrin Hatch fleeing an interview in disgust. Bonds was one of a kind. He also made news because of his relationship with alcohol.

If you think that diminished his attitude or his demeanor...then you're not from Detroit. Although he failed in trying to make it in larger markets like New York or Los Angeles, here...he was sometimes referred to as the "Sun King" in the newspapers, presumably because of his ratings that were touted to be as much of 50% of the total viewing audience. When Bonds was away during a stint in rehab, our numbers were down. When he returned, they were up again. People tuned in to see what he would say, or do next. On one such occasion, he was rumored to have received a raise upon his return.

My introduction to Bonds happened when I met him on the set of his 5:00 news broadcast. The setting only included a simple round table….about four feet across. He leaned in with the cameras rolling and said, "If (name a team. I can't remember which) wins, I'll get you some bar-b-que and some red pop to go with it." The suggestive racist overtones were as obvious as the color of my skin. I wasn't going to give him the satisfaction of becoming upset. I told him I would make the correct call regarding the event/game, so bring me the 'que and the red pop too. He said, "I can't get next to you." I said to him, as we continued the "live" broadcast, "I'm not sure what you mean"…but again requested him to be sure and bring me that red pop too!

THE LIONS ARE CHAMPIONS!

From a sportscaster's perspective, Detroit offers so many memories! The teams, the players…and those 1983 NFC Central Champion Lions! I know you probably forgot about them. And the fact they were coming off a visit to the playoffs in 1982, does little to help your recollection, unless you played for the team, were one of those crazy fans, or you are a trivia buff.

First, there was a strike that year. It cut the regular season from 16 to 9 games. But they would make the playoffs…with a losing record! One of only four teams to get into the post season with more losses than wins. Four up and five down. More trivia? The Lions and Cleveland Browns are the only wildcard representatives to do that. By the way, the Lions would lose to the Washington Redskins 31-7 to end the year.

In 1983, their one and four start gave little hope that another trip to the playoffs was possible. The offense was sporadic, but they had a defense. Doug English and William Gay were sack-masters. English had 13 and Gay 13 ½. Eric Hipple was good and bad at quarterback.

He would throw for almost 2,600 yards, but for only 12 touchdowns. Then there were those 18 interceptions. Billy Sims missed four games because of an injury, but still gained over a thousand yards on the ground. Fullback James Jones delivered almost a thousand yards... half coming from 46 receptions.

The Lions would close out the year just the opposite of the way they started, four wins and one loss. They could wrap up the NFC Central with a win or a loss by Green Bay. Both scenarios would come true as Gary Danielson substituted for an injured Hipple, in a 23-20 victory...and the Bears beat the Packers 23-21.

Again Danielson would start at quarterback, this time against San Francisco. He suffered five interceptions, four in the first half. The defense stood tall, as it had all season. Eddie Murray's 54-yard field goal, a playoff record, kept the Lions close, 14-9 at intermission. Billy Sims had 114 yards rushing and a couple of fourth quarter touchdowns. But Joe Montana delivered what he is known for, late game theatrics. He hit Freddie Solomon for a touchdown with 1:23 left, as San Francisco reclaimed the lead, 24-23.

The Lions didn't fold: but with Head Coach Monte Clark looking skyward, his hands together, literally praying with five seconds left on the game clock, the man we had come to know as "Eddie Money", missed from 43 yards out. Detroit loses by one. It was the first divisional championship game since 1957. The team wouldn't return to the postseason for eight years.

NUMBER 20 IS DONE

That was a tough way to end the year, but next season it would be the end of a career for Billy Sims. He was the one person the franchise could ill-afford to lose. He was a Heisman Trophy winner, the first overall pick in the 1980 draft and he made the Pro Bowl in each of his first three seasons. Sims was simply the heart, soul, and ego of the Lions. With Sims on the field, they knew victory was a definite possibility.

He would do all he could for sure, whether it was delivering a leaping karate kick that would have made Bruce Lee proud, or a spinning, bull-like run that would have impressed Jim Brown.

But now Sims is done...and for that matter so are the Lions as a team, including Head Coach Monte Clark and his staff. The Lions finished the year 4-11 and 1.

It started with a simple sweep right in Minnesota. Sims had been complaining about the turf...saying he thought it was bad at the Silverdome, but the Metrodome had to be worse. Sims got his foot caught in the surface, then was tackled. He said it wasn't a direct hit on his knees, but his right knee suffered multiple ligament damage. The surface of the knee joint also was injured. Sims vowed he would be ready in '85 and later said the same thing regarding a possible return in 1989. It made for good conversation, but despite his best of intentions, it didn't happen.

Sims only played for four and a half years, but still sits as the Lions second all-time rusher, behind another number 20, Hall of Famer Barry Sanders. Sims rushed for 5,106 yards during his professional career and scored 42 touchdowns.

CHUCK WHO?

From the gridiron to the hardwood, the flip was made at the Pontiac Silverdome for ten years. The Lions would leave and the Pistons would enter, but in 1983 they were also bringing a new head coach as well... Charles Jerome Daly. The Pistons would never be the same.

Scotty Robertson was shown the exit after only 37 wins in 1982-83. Those victories were two less than the previous year. Still, Robertson was fairly popular when you consider he finished in third place during back to back seasons. But Pistons General Manager, Jack McCloskey, had enough. He was bringing in Chuck Daly, who had been fired in Cleveland at the end of the '82 campaign.

Many fans of the Pistons were upset and they were voicing their displeasure rather loudly. Chuck who? Which I felt was a legitimate question. Daly's resume was highlighted by success at Punxsutawney High School and the University of Pennsylvania, but this was the National Basketball Association. Chuck's only attempt on this level was his 9 and 32 record in Cleveland and he was fired.

So, I relayed on camera what was being said by some fans. Chuck who? It wasn't what I was asking, it was the fans. As soon as I finished that broadcast I got a call from McCloskey. I think he would have choked me had he been in my presence. He was furious. He said I didn't know what I was talking about. I tried to explain it wasn't me saying Chuck who? It was the fans. I invited him to join me the next day on my 6:00 sportscast and we could talk this thing out. He was not having any of that, he said. McCloskey left me with a few more choice words, then hung up the phone.

Wow...I didn't expect this. Usually if a high level management-type has a disagreement, he'll corner you at practice. Apparently Jack couldn't wait. In fact neither could Chuck Daly, because he contacted me shortly after Jack McCloskey. Chuck was willing to join me in the studio. This spoke volumes about him, and it was smart because Chuck was very personable. Plus he had that kind of smile that left you wondering if there was more to whatever he was thinking or saying.

I thought we cleared everything up and had a great relationship during his nine year stay in Detroit. But surprise, surprise...when his book, "Daly Life" came out, on page 86 he writes..."Jay Berry said on the air, Who is this guy? Chuck who?"

I just shook my head and laughed because I had been misinterpreted. But it makes for a good story whether I tell it...or he does.

World Champion Tigers

In 1984 The Detroit Tigers came out swinging and never stopped. Like a buzz- saw to plywood...the opposition didn't stand a chance. Had it been a championship bout, it would have ended seconds into the fight. They were simply incredible! At the time, they were one of only three teams in the history of Major League Baseball to lead from start to finish. But in reality, the ground work was laid the year before by finishing 22 games above .500 and runner-up to the Baltimore Orioles. No need for wholesale changes, just a tweak here…by signing Darrell Evans as a free agent, and a tweak there…by picking up Willie Hernandez and Dave Bergman in a trade with Philadelphia in exchange for John Wockenfuss and Glenn Wilson. They were ready to roll…all the way to the championship.

Even today it is hard to comprehend that 35-5 start, which included 17 consecutive victories on the road. Jack Morris had already thrown a no-hitter, and minus a towering blast over the right field roof by Reggie Jackson, opposing teams had little to celebrate. These were noteworthy performances. Since our competitor, WDIV-TV, was televising the games and had come up with a catchy slogan, "Bless You Boys"…we needed a presence, especially on the road out west.

We were turning down trips right and left. Travel is sort of a payoff for reporters/anchors if you are normally attached to a studio chair and covering routine stories. On the road you know you will be spotlighted, because the station is not sending you there for nothing. You will work, maybe delivering live shots at noon, five, six and eleven. But again you are part of the action…on the scene. However, these incredible Tigers were starting to wear even us down. The comfort of home was beginning to look very appealing…after all, baseball has a long season.

Being with the team does offer the opportunity to get to know the players and management better. I recall in Oakland, Kirk Gibson was acting overly pleasant prior to a game. I had picked up a crew from our sister station in San Francisco. Cheaper to fly and house just me…and not have to pay for a full crew. Anyway, we couldn't shake Gibson. He kept popping up where ever we went.

This was not like him. He wasn't usually about chit-chat, but today he was. Then I figured it out. Part of the crew I was working with included a young lady who was wearing jeans and a top that was part of a one-piece bathing suit! So that's why he was following us around like a puppy. Gibson could have saved his nice guy routine, she had eyes for Dan Petry, who didn't appear to know she existed. That was funny!

Gibson had an edge about him (outside of the aforementioned story) and so did Jack Morris. But I could approach Jack and get what I needed for a story, but that wasn't a sure thing with Gibson. He could be a challenge.

I knew Chet Lemon from Chicago when he was roaming center field for the White Sox. I got to know him better when he joined the Tigers and learned he could be quite the jokester. I recall being in a bank drive-through line and was startled when someone, on the blind side of my car, suddenly jumped up yelling "BOO!" He scared me to death and had the biggest laugh from the encounter. Even today, when in a similar situation, I constantly check to see if someone is creeping around. Thanks Chet, you rascal you!

Dave Bergman was another favorite of mine. Our conversations usually involved more than baseball. A true gentleman and a nice, nice man. Fortunately, the same can be said for the squad as a whole, including: Alan Trammell, "Sweet Lou" Whitaker, Lance Parrish, Milt Wilcox, Dan Petry, Tom Brookens, Darrell Evans, Willie Hernandez, and manager Sparky Anderson, of course…all the way down the roster. Their professional approach made our jobs easier, and of course, winning makes everything better.

And win they did…with everyone contributing. Barbaro Garbey, Ruppert Jones, and Rusty Kuntz shared the media attention. Marty Castillo was also a factor at third base, as a backup catcher and offensively with his bat.

Sparky had a squad to meet all possible challenges and he celebrated with the rest of the team, as the Tigers captured the American League East crown on September 18th. Eleven days later, they enjoyed one of many milestones, by picking up win number 104, a franchise record.

The inevitable had been achieved, now for the fun stuff…the post season. First up, the Kansas City Royals in the American League

Championship Series. It was pretty much like the regular season. The pitching staff, led by Jack Morris, Dan Petry, Milt Wilcox, and Willie Hernandez kept the Royals in check. Offensively, big hits came from throughout the lineup. Gibson is named MVP of the series. The Royals fought hard, but are swept three games to none.

The San Diego Padres would join the Tigers in the World Series. Midwest fans were hoping for an I-94 series showdown with the Chicago Cubs. They did win the National League East title, but after jumping out to a two games to none advantage against San Diego in the National League Championship Series, the Cubs had to leave the friendly confines of Wrigley Field. The Padres caught fire in San Diego and won the next three, setting up the matchup with Detroit.

This would be the first World Series for the Tigers since the historic showdown with the St. Louis Cardinals in 1968. Anticipation was high, anxiety as well. Could the Tigers find a way to add another pennant to their storied franchise, or be left thinking what could've, or should have been? The competition would start in San Diego.

The Padres led it two to one against Jack Morris until the fifth, when Larry Herndon hit a two-out, two run homerun. Morris, who went the distance, did not allow another run to score and the Tigers won it three to two.

The Padres would take game two, thanks to Kurt Bevacqua's three-run homerun off Dan Petry. It was San Diego's first franchise victory in a World Series, five to three the final. So the faithful in Detroit clung to hope that a change in scenery would turn the tide, as the action moved to Tiger Stadium. They would not be disappointed.

The Tigers exploded with four runs in the second, including two on a home run by Marty Castillo, while San Diego started to unravel. Padres' pitchers issued 11 walks in the first five innings. Milt Wilcox and the Tigers enjoy a five to two victory.

Game four became a highlight reel for Alan Trammel, who supplied all the offense necessary for Detroit, thanks to a couple of two-run shots into the seats. Jack Morris picks up his second series victory and second complete game. Tigers take a four to two decision, and look to close it out in game five.

The Tigers light the scoreboard with three runs in the first, but the Padres rally to tie it in the fourth. Then things got interesting in the eighth. The Tigers lead it five to four and have runners at second and third, with one out. Padres' manager Dick Williams called on hard throwing Goose Gossage to walk Kirk Gibson and set up a possible double play, or at least a force out at the plate. Gibson had already hit a homerun in the first inning off Mark Thurmond.

The situation becomes the pivotal moment of the entire series. Gossage shook off Williams' sign to walk Gibson. Sparky yells from the Tigers' dugout…"They don't want to walk you,"…meaning Gossage thinks he can strike out Gibby. Williams goes to the mound where Gossage says, "Let's go after him." Gibson would later explain, "Gossage owned me and he struck me out in my first major league at bat. He threw hard, and I swung hard, and he was just one of those guys who gave me trouble. I knew he thought he could strike me out again."

While Gibson is watching the conference on the mound between Gossage and Williams, he says he went into a positive visualization mode. Thinking to himself it's time for a change in his battles with Gossage. "I'm thinking I'm going to get you when it counts and it counts right now." So the stage was set for one of the most memorable "at bats" in Tigers history.

With the crowd buzzing, Gossage sent Gibson an outside fast ball. The next throw was what the Tigers' outfielder was waiting for, and Gibson's celebration of outstretched arms over his head, and him deliriously screaming…tells the story. He delivered a three run blast into the upper deck in right; sending his team, the crowd, and all of Detroit for that matter…into the kind of all-consuming euphoria that's only heard and seen during moments like this.

Tigers win the game eight to four….and the series five games to one. But the celebration in the streets around Tiger Stadium was downright scary. Like Gibson's photograph of jubilation, there is another of a "fan" if you will, Kenneth (Bubba) Helms, reportedly an eighth grade dropout from Lincoln Park...holding a Tigers World Series pennant. Behind him is an overturned car that has been set on fire. That picture circulated across the nation, in newspapers and magazines. Another photo shows a half dozen men trying to turn over a Checker Cab. The company's offices were across the street from the stadium. The final Associated Press numbers from the "celebration" were...34 arrests (few had attended the game), one dead, dozens injured. I happened to be off that day and attended the game. I couldn't get out of there fast enough...it truly was crazy!

Some other numbers of note from the season...Sparky Anderson is the American League Manager of the year, Kirk Gibson is the American League Championship Series Most Valuable Player, and Willie Hernandez...who found no love in Chicago when I was working there, is the American League Cy Young Award Winner, American League MVP, and The Sporting News Pitcher of the Year.

1984 Olympic Gold

The Tigers weren't the only ones slugging their way to a crown during the summer of '84. Detroit...known for being a boxing mecca since the days of the great Joe Louis, had a couple of local contenders hunting gold in the Los Angeles Olympics.

Steve McCrory, a fast talking flyweight, was the younger brother of Milton McCrory. Milton eventually captured the World Boxing Council Welterweight title. In addition to a gold medal, Steve was hoping to launch his own successful pro career, using the summer games as his launching pad. He was aided by a boycott that included the Soviet Union, Eastern Germany, and Cuba. Still, Steve had taken a bronze medal a year earlier at the '83 Pan Am games, which made the L.A. Coliseum a definite stop during our two weeks of covering the competition in Los Angeles.

McCrory, like his older brother, would box for the legendary Kronk gym. He didn't have any problems during the preliminary rounds of the championship, and easily took home the gold medal. But his hope of turning his success into a pro title didn't materialize. He was 35 and 0, when he ran out of gas against Jeff Fenech during an International Boxing Federation bantamweight title match. After McCrory suffered the 14th round technical knockout, his career never really bounced back. Steve passed away in 2000 at the age of 36, following a prolonged illness.

Frank Tate, a light middleweight from Detroit, would also breeze through the Olympics. He started with a couple of 5-0 decisions, stopped another opponent in the first round, and advanced in the quarterfinals because of a medical issue with his next challenger. Tate then defeated Shawn O'Sullivan of Canada in the finals, 5-0 and won the Gold medal.

He was expected to stick with Kronk as a pro, but reportedly turned down an offer from trainer Emanuel Steward, the head of the Kronk gym. According to Tate, Steward's offer was a $90,000 house and a new Pontiac with one catch...Emanuel's name would be on both the house and car.

Instead, Tate decided to leave Detroit and sign with Houston Boxing Association (HBA) in December of '84. He would capture the vacant IBF crown in 1987, but issues with his weight became a problem, and he would lose his title to southpaw Michael Nunn. Later, Tate lost a couple of championship fights to Virgil Hill, his former teammate in the '84 Olympics. He would continue to box until 1998, but following a loss to David Telesco, he decided to retire with a professional record of 41-5, with 24 knockouts.

THE MCGEE TWINS AND GLADYS KNIGHT

I absolutely love the Olympics, especially the Summer Olympics. "The thrill of victory and the agony of defeat" as ABC's Jim McKay used to say, during the opening of the "Wide World of Sports" program. During the Olympics, invariably you couldn't help but be drawn to the compelling human interest part of the competition. Kudos to those broadcasting the games, because that is something that they have mastered.

During the 1984 Olympics, the story of Paula and Pamela McGee caught my attention on many levels. First they were from Flint, Michigan...just 68 miles Northwest of Detroit. They had guided Flint Northern High School, the Lady Vikings, to back to back state Class A Basketball Championships in 1978 and 1979. They were tall, 6'4". They excelled on the track team...shot put, high jump, quarter mile, and relays. They served as president of their high school class. They were easy on the eyes and they were good enough to get scholarships to the University of Southern California, where with Cheryl Miller, they were major components for the Trojans' 1983 and '84 NCAA national titles. They were All-America, and both set numerous records. They were inseparable until it came to choosing the 1984 Olympic squad. Pam made the team, Paula did not.

The U.S. women crushed their opposition. An opening round 83-55 decision is the closest it would get. The gold medal game was a 30-point blowout of South Korea...85-55.

The medal ceremony still provides me with a smile...and a tear. It was magic and heartwarming as Pam, after receiving her medal, sought out Paula in the crowd in the Los Angeles Forum, then placed her gold medal around her sisters' neck and embraced her. Cue the tears and there were plenty. It was a spontaneous, loving gesture—one that touched a nation. The kind of moment I had been waiting for.

Months prior to this, I discovered a performance by Gladys Knight that I put away just for something like this. I liked, under the right circumstances, to put music with my reports to illustrate and enhance what I was trying to communicate. Back then you were not restricted in how much of the music could be used. Last I checked that is no longer the case.

Larry Henley and Jeff Silbar wrote "Wind Beneath My Wings", for Bette Midler who sang it in the movie "Beaches." It was a No.1 hit in 1989 and Midler captured the Grammy Award for record of the year. Gladys Knight's version is super soulful and was perfect for my report.

"Wind Beneath My Wings"

Jeff Silbar and Larry Henley

It must have been cold there in my shadow, to never have sunlight on your face. You were content to let me shine, that's your way. You always walked a step behind.

So I was the one with all the glory, while you were the one with all the strength. A beautiful face without a name for so long. A beautiful smile to hide the pain.

Did you ever know that you're my hero, and everything I would like to be? I can fly higher than an eagle, 'cause you are the wind beneath my wings.

Beautiful, beautiful song. With the pictures from the medal ceremony, I knew it would be a memorable report. It was, except when it was broadcast, I didn't get any credit for producing it!

I was talked into allowing it to be run during our 11:00 newscast, of which I wasn't a part. I was anchoring the 6:00. We needed to have another "piece" run from the Olympics, and as a "team player", I permitted my report to be broadcast at 11:00. On a story like this, you didn't need anyone's voice, unless it was Pam's or Paula's. I let the pictures and music deliver the emotion, the story if you will. Since I had planned to run it on the show I would be anchoring, it all just made sense.

You could tell by the looks on the faces of Bill Bonds and Diana Lewis that they were blown away, and they expressed as much. The sports anchor that night, my "teammate", took in all the accolades while sitting on the studio set, when it was obvious this wasn't his style of reporting! You don't suddenly become something you're not. If you're a dog...you can't turn into a cat. If you're a horse...how can you become a cow? But never once did he say that this was my work... that I produced it!

The pats on the back continued. When I arrived the next day I was furious and asked him when was he going to acknowledge that I was the one who produced the report? He looked as if he had been caught...but his response was not memorable.

Competition is a driving force in many jobs. Sports, sales, information technology, design engineering, financial planning...all are extremely competitive. But getting one's "mug" on that camera, and keeping it there, doesn't take a back seat to any of them. I believe it led to what happened to me. Whether on the football field, basketball court, or in front of the camera...if I wasn't good enough, my goal was to get better. But I am not naïve and realize not everybody thinks that way, especially in television.

THE MAKING OF THE BAD BOYS

The Detroit sports scene, which has always provided plenty to talk about, was getting ready to take us to unexplored places, thanks to the Pistons. Chuck Daly's cupboard wasn't exactly bare when he inherited that '82-'83 squad. He had Isiah Lord Thomas, the third...to run the show. Isiah was good enough to have been the second overall selection in the 1981 National Basketball Association draft, right behind his good buddy Mark Aguirre. Their agent, George Andrews, was my neighbor in Chicago.

While George never discussed information regarding his clients with me, I realized that suddenly Isiah and Mark were basically living in our high-rise, prior to the draft. I also had heard that Isiah had no desire to go to Dallas, which had the first pick. Mark, word had it, didn't have a preference. So George, who was agent for both Mark and Isiah, couldn't lose. Aguirre was selected first and Isiah second, allowing him to remain just 282 miles from his hometown... Chicago.

Isiah didn't disappoint. He made the All-Rookie squad and started for the Eastern Conference in the 1982 All-Star game, even though the Pistons were a below .500 team. Another thing, Daly was known for playing tough defense, it was his strong suit. The way this team was setup, it was basically trying to outscore opponents.

Daly brought in Dick Harter to help concentrate on defense. In the meantime, and I think this was important, Chuck Daly tried to get to know his players. It sounds simple, but too many coaches have in their mind how they want to do things, rather than playing to their strengths. If your milk has spoiled and you want an omelet, how about using sour cream as a substitute? Consider Daly a chef...a little bit of this and a whole lot of that. He knew what he wanted, or what he thought his recipe called for, but where humans are concerned...sometimes you may never know, until it's too late...and it blows up in your face. There are no guarantees, especially in the NBA.

According to his book, *Daly Life*, before he could focus on his players, Daly also knew his relationship with McCloskey could become an issue. Daly sensed that McCloskey, one of the toughest competitors he's known in basketball, still wanted to be a coach at times. In fact, Daly had been warned that his general manager will want to have some input beyond his front office duties. So Daly gave an assistant the responsibility of dealing with Jack, then relay any necessary information back to him. Some of it Daly rejected, and some he accepted, but it worked out well because both Irishmen wanted to win.

Win they did. The Pistons finished with 12 more victories than the previous season and came within a game of taking the central division. The next two years the team finished with identical records of 46 and 36, and again in second place in the division. In his fourth season, Daly and the Pistons traded Earl Cureton and a second round pick to Chicago, for Sidney Green. But more importantly, Kelly Tripucka and Kent Benson were sent to Utah for Adrian Dantley, and a couple of draft choices.

While the record book showed improvement, it was another second place in the division for the team. However, in the playoffs it was obvious things were changing. They easily whipped Atlanta in five games, this after finishing five games behind the Hawks in the regular season.

Isiah owned that series, averaging 27 points a game. The Pistons were starting to make their climb up the NBA ladder and people were starting to take notice. Especially out at the cavernous Pontiac Silverdome, where attendance was over 22,000 per game and climbing. Over 38,000 watched a contest against Chicago in February. Next up…another rung on that ladder, the defending NBA Champion Boston Celtics!

The Pistons Climb MT. Boston

During the regular season, Boston prevailed three games to one. The Pistons split at home and were looking for their first victory in Bean Town. Good thing the Bad Boys were loved at home, because they were hated everywhere else. They could have cared less. Their nickname was well earned, and they wore it like their favorite shirt…as often as possible. Drive down the middle of the lane, and you will pay dearly for the privilege. Battle for a rebound, and risk the consequences. It didn't matter who you were…or who you thought you were, no exemptions. Bill Laimbeer no longer had to do all of the dirty work. Rick Mahorn had joined the team, along with Dennis Rodman and John Salley. That quartet spelled pain and misery for opponents.

The stage is set for one of the most memorable playoff series in modern history. The fans in the Boston Garden were ready to deliver some intimidation of their own, hoping to turn the tables on those thugs from Detroit. Boston, as expected would take the first two and send the action to the Silverdome. The Pistons would blitz Boston with 37 points in the first quarter and never look back in game three.

As a preview of things to come, Laimbeer slams Larry Bird to the ground during a fight for a rebound. Both are kicked out of the game and fined. $5,000 for Laimbeer...$2,000 for Bird. 122-104 are the most important numbers for the Pistons and their fans. They get better as the Pistons shame the Celtics 145-119 in game four, sending the series back to Boston tied at two.

Outside of the Pistons hotel prior to game five, a large crowd has gathered, and one observer said "Maybe they're waiting for Bill Laimbeer." "No," replied a Celtics fan..."they're not armed."

Payback can be many things....supplied in many different ways, but what happened to Laimbeer, whether you love him or hate him, was just WRONG in capital letters. Just before half-time of game five...during a tight contest, Robert Parrish, repeatedly hits Laimbeer while fighting for a rebound. Laimbeer is floored by the assault, and not one call. Nothing from the zebras or the league. As if that wasn't enough vindication for what happened to Bird in game three, he steals an inbound pass from Isiah with five seconds remaining, throws it to Dennis Johnson for a winning layup. 108-107 Boston and a three-two series lead for the Celtics as the action returns to the Pontiac Silverdome.

Vinnie Johnson, Adrian Dantley and Isiah all score 21 or more points in game six, to offset 35 by Bird. Pistons send it back to Boston tied at three, thanks to a 113-105 victory. However, a trip to the NBA finals proves elusive as Dantley and Vinnie Johnson collide...head-on, while chasing a loose ball in the third quarter. Dantley is carried off on a stretcher and V.J. is ineffective, mainly nursing his wounds with an ice pack for the remainder of game seven. Joe Dumars had his best game, scoring 35, Isiah 25. Bird had 37 points, nine rebounds, and nine assists...as all the Celtics starters finish in double figures. The Pistons fall short 117-114 and Boston advances to meet the L.A. Lakers.

But the drama from this series wasn't over...hardly. Dennis Rodman, during post-game interviews, claimed that Bird gets notice and awards largely because he is White. "He's White...that's the only reason he gets it," Rodman said. "I think he's very overrated." Isiah added "I think Larry is a very, very good basketball player. He's an exceptional talent. But I have to agree with Rodman. If he were Black he'd be just another good guy."

Isiah later, allegedly, claimed he was misquoted. But there was a recording, reportedly, that proved differently. Eventually Isiah, with the urging of Pistons management, sought out Bird, met and talked it out. A national news conference followed, in which Bird defused the controversy by saying the remarks didn't bother him, so why should they bother anyone else? That told me a lot about Larry Bird that day. Not many people, Black or White, are mature and sensitive enough to do what he did. Hats off to number 33…a man's man!

This bothered me because Isiah and I had formed a bond, or so I thought and this just wasn't like Isiah. I still like him, although we haven't talked in years. Early in his career and shortly after my arrival in Detroit, it was nothing for me to grab a camera crew, and go to his home and just rap…about anything, or Isiah would sometimes join me on the set in the studio. He meant…and I'm sure still means a lot to this city and area. I recall him organizing "No Crime Day" that brought together thousands…Black and White. I don't know what was going on following the loss in game seven…but I was stunned and not able to get clarification because of my commitments to deliver reports on Channel 7. Like others, I was left shaking my head and wondering…what that was all about. If I had to guess, I think it was the heat of the moment, following a hard fought loss and microphones being everywhere.

Often I hear youngsters in particular, talk about what their plans are for the future: the kind of life they want to live, the car they will drive, the home they hope to own, etc. I smile and reflect back to my own life. Who knows, besides God, what the future holds? I, fortunately or unfortunately, couldn't plan beyond the present. I didn't have a clue, because until I reached my teens I had no ambitions. I guess there is nothing wrong with contemplating your next step, because it could lead to a successful life. However, what if you fail along the way, how will that be handled? What if your ambition ends up being less desirable as you mature?

These thoughts come to mind when I see athletes, having achieved their objective of becoming a professional, suddenly realize how much is required to reach the ultimate goal, a championship. It is hard...real hard to capture and it's where the Pistons find themselves heading into the 1987-88 season.

They had overcome Bernard King and the New York Knicks, but not before losing an incredible duel between Isiah and King in the first round of the 1984 playoffs. In the deciding game five, Isiah scored an unbelievable 16 points in the last 1:34 to force overtime. But King and the Knicks prevailed and eliminated the Pistons, three games to one. The Celtics sent New York home, four games to two, in the '85 Eastern Conference Semifinals. In the 1986 playoffs, Dominique Wilkens, "the Human Highlight Reel," and the Atlanta Hawks knocked off the Pistons, three games to one.

Now Boston was the obstacle again. I think about what Bo Schembechler used to say "We don't rebuild….we reload!" The Pistons appear to be following that blue print. This year they add 7-foot center James "Buddha" Edwards to their arsenal. Chuck Daly coached Edwards in Cleveland and anxiously looked forward to the reunion. Many nights the Pistons would ride the Buddha train to victory, delighting the Bad Boys faithful in the process.

The Pistons finished first in the Central. They advanced past the Washington Bullets in the first round of the playoffs, three games to two. Michael Jordan and the Chicago Bulls weren't ready to realistically challenge, and would lose four games to one. That set the stage for what the Pistons had pointed toward since the previous monumental struggle with Boston.

The series would open in the Garden. Isiah and the Pistons were ready. Zeke, as Isiah was known, dropped 35 on the Celtics, and in so doing delivered a major change in the script by winning 104-96. It was the first victory in Bean Town for the Bad Boys after suffering 21 straight losses. This time the Celtics had nothing to stop the inevitable. The Pistons' success on defense was most telling on Bird, whose scoring average dipped below 20 points a game, forcing Boston to rely more on Kevin McHale. Meanwhile, Isiah got help from everyone…Dantley, Dumars, Laimbeer, and Vinnie Johnson, "the Microwave," all average double figures during the series, won by the Pistons four games to two. Finally they have reached the top of the Eastern Conference, but the "Magic Man" and the Lakers await…out in La La land.

The Pistons Vs. Showtime

This was also a pivotal point for me as a sportscaster. It will be my first pro basketball championship series. This is big for everyone associated with the confrontation: the teams, fans, reporters and their respective stations, newspapers and magazines included. There are people from all over the world interested and because of all the attention, just getting basic information and covering the games and practices become tougher.

Many times you are herded like cattle into news conferences, stepping around cameras, microphones, and wires…and there are not that many one on one opportunities. Its exciting work but very stressful. The competition is at its peak. You don't want to be scooped. Like the players, it's time to be at the top of your game. Folks sitting at home might be wishing they could be in my shoes…but in reality they have no clue what I am having to deal with. But like their favorite meal, they want it to taste like they expect, they don't care about the sweat that went into making it. So no sympathy and I can't blame them.

The Lakers and Celtics have dominated the post season for years, meaning the Pistons are definite underdogs and won't be given anything…especially in the way of calls. It's just the way it is and is evident as the series progresses. Not that the Lakers need help. They are the defending champs and following a championship parade the previous season, Pat Riley has already predicted another title this year.

The 1988 series started with a famous kiss on the cheek between Isiah and Earvin "Magic" Johnson, but their friendship quickly deteriorated as the series unfolded. It would start at the Fabulous Forum which was full of Hollywood notables who had become familiar with what was fittingly called, "Showtime." Earvin, a 6'9" guard from Michigan State, dazzled and amazed with his flashy no look passes and ball handling. He fueled the Lakers offense and thrilled the crowd. He had been doing it since outdueling Larry Bird and Indiana State in the 1979 NCAA Championship game. Magic had help too...Kareem Abdul Jabbar, James Worthy, Michael Cooper, A.C. Green, Byron Scott, Mychal Thompson, and Kurt Rambis among others.

But Isiah and the Pistons served notice by taking game one, 105-93. Adrian Dantley missed only two shots from the field and just one free throw, while scoring 34 points. The media in Los Angeles thought the Lakers, like the Celtics before them, looked old compared to these hungry, defensive-minded Pistons. But Chuck Daly knew game two would be decidedly different and he was right. The Lakers, who felt humiliated after the opener, won game two, 108-96.

Over 39,000, a playoff record in the NBA, greeted the Pistons and Lakers for the third game of the series. The Pontiac Silverdome, which was built for football, is an interesting venue for basketball, to say the least. A section is separated from the rest of the 80,000 seat stadium, by what look like huge curtains or drapes, if you will. In the middle is a basketball court. I'm surprised that more players didn't complain about sight issues, when shooting in such a large arena. I felt the same about the Houston Astrodome. But this was home for the Pistons (The Palace would open next year) and they knew the best spots to shoot from, to escape the glare of the huge stadium lights.

Turns out the Lakers had no problem with the 'dome either. They outscored the Pistons 31-14 in the third period...breaking open what had been a one point game, to win game three...99-86. The Lakers were feeling confident, and the Pistons, for the first time in a while... like they were actually beaten, and had not given the game away.

With the shift to Michigan came the two-three-two playoff format. So, although Los Angeles led the series two to one, the Pistons could still salvage a three-two advantage by winning the next two at the Silverdome. That's what they did.

Dantley's 27 points, combined with bench scoring from Vinnie Johnson and James Edwards, provided the offense the Pistons needed. It helped put Magic Johnson in early foul trouble and made for an easy win for Detroit 111-86, tying the series at two. L.A. opened game five by scoring the first 12 points and uncharacteristically, tried to be the aggressor or so it appeared…and it backfired. Dantley had 19 of his 25 in the first half, Dumars threw in 19 and Vinnie 16 off the bench. 104-94 Pistons the final, as they and their fans wave a solemn good bye to the Silverdome, and brace for a return to the Forum. Whatever the future held would be decided there.

A win in the next two contests and Detroit would have its first NBA title in the history of its franchise. The Pistons took game one in L.A., so the possibility of it happening again wasn't unthinkable…but the sooner the better. Detroit trailed by eight in the third, when Isiah exploded for 14 straight points. He was the smallest player on the court, yet bigger than anyone at the most critical moments. Zeke was always the hero riding to the rescue.

But wait! He is suddenly on the floor in obvious pain and needs help getting up and to the bench. Isiah had severely sprained his ankle after landing on Michael Cooper's foot. The Pistons' captain willed his way back onto the court and continued to put on a display, with a national audience wincing with his every move. His 25 points in the quarter, were the most ever in a finals competition. The Pistons led by two heading to the fourth.

Fast forward…just a minute left to play, Pistons 102, Lakers 99. Byron Scott scores for L.A. which pulled to within one…52 seconds left. Isiah proved human when he missed a jumper. 14 ticks remaining, and this is the play that will forever haunt Detroit. Kareem sets up along the baseline for his classic sky-hook with Laimbeer guarding. Kareem misses…but the official, unbelievably whistles Laimbeer for a foul. He never touched him!!! It took Pat Riley, the Lakers coach,

30 years before he admitted it was a blown call. Kareem calmly sinks both free throws giving L.A. a 103-102 advantage. It held up when Dennis Rodman couldn't rebound a Dumars miss. There will be a game seven and discussion for decades about that bad call and Isiah's amazing effort...43-points, eight assists and six steals. But was it wasted? That question wouldn't be answered for a couple of days as trainer Mike Abdenour tried to put Isiah back together again.

It was obvious during the pre-game warmups that Isiah was in bad shape, as he limped around the court. He helped secure a five point half-time advantage but his ankle became worse in the second half. The Lakers opened up a sizeable lead and held on for a three point victory, 108-105...and as Riley had predicted, their second straight Championship. The Pistons had taken another step up the NBA ladder, but knew they should've been the team celebrating... two days ago.

THEM AGAINST THE WORLD

"FIGHT THE POWER, FIGHT THE POWER...WE GOTTA FIGHT THE POWER THAT BE." The driving beat...the booming bass and the repetitive lyrics "FIGHT THE POWER, FIGHT THE POWER THAT BE"... engulfs everybody.

Welcome to the Pistons locker room, brought to you in part by the rap group Public Enemy. The team...and its audible and visual theme, is a quick indication you've entered a different world. It's not for the faint of heart! You are surrounded by giants, and you better stand taller than you ever have. Not one flinch, no indication that there is an ounce of wimp in you, or you will be embarrassed.

Questions of how is your morning going? Might return a reply like "what the_____ do you want..." and possibly followed by, "I'm not answering any more damn questions." And this was one of their better days.

Like their treatment of the opposing team, the Bad Boys would test you...see what you were made of. It didn't matter if previously, I had what I thought was a decent and productive interview. Today was a different day. Yet, I still had a job to do and didn't want to make a potentially explosive encounter worse. Sometimes I would meet their surliness with a matter of fact demeanor and show I was about business; or I might try a different tactic, a stare-down…without saying a word, not immediately, or I would laugh off their bluster. But whatever I did, I didn't want to try flattery…they would see right through it, and in not the nicest language, let me know it.

I usually got what I needed. What may have started as a contentious encounter, ended with laughter…often at my own expense. But there was many a wide-eyed reporter, who left their lockers muttering to themselves and wondering, what was that all about?

From General Manager Jack McCloskey, to head coach Chuck Daly…on down their ranks, the Pistons were a tough group…for the most part. John "Spider" Salley was the jokester and could lighten any situation. He was an entertainer and never saw a microphone he didn't like. Joe "D" Dumars was always someone I could count on to help me out with an interview, and James Edwards was another who would often take the time to give me what I needed.

Adrian "A.D." Dantley didn't appear to like doing interviews. His eyes would often dart around his surroundings. He seemed to want to be someplace else when he had a microphone in his face. With Bill "Laim" Laimbeer, you could be cut off mid-sentence with "That's a stupid question, next question." Sometimes he was right, it was a stupid question from a reporter and sometimes he was wrong. I found him most approachable in the off season, away from the arena, where he was always wearing his game face.

Rick "Horn" Mahorn was the biggest, and most caring teddy bear. Which is usually after he's intimidated you to the point of you being ready to look elsewhere for an interview. He is still one of my favorites. Dennis "Worm" Rodman was extremely emotional and being held in check by the veterans at this point of his career.

With Isiah, the most popular player, it just depended on how many interviews he had already done, and how many were lined up in front of his locker to do more. I felt his pain and didn't approach him during those moments, unless I had to.

Yes, they could be bad to the bone, and some even called them dirty. While all of their actions weren't condoned, they brought pride to Detroit and all of Michigan for that matter, along with a blue collar work ethic and an extra helping of resiliency. You didn't have to love 'em...but you would think twice before taking it down the middle. 'Nuff said.

Dunk you Very Much!

"Dunk you very much!" was a catch phrase I started using to describe some of the action that was part of my highlights during my sportscasts. Imagine my surprise when it started showing up on SportsCenter, and later as part of a marketing campaign by Nike. I was stunned! So were fans of the Pistons, but for a different reason, when word surfaced about a deal that would forever change the complexion of the team.

For months McCloskey and Daly discussed a potential trade that would send Adrian Dantley, the team's leading scorer during the previous season and the Championship series against the Lakers, to Dallas for Mark Aguirre. The risk was huge, but the Pistons considered the potential rewards worth it.

Aguirre was having his problems in Dallas and after Dantley got into a shouting match with Daly during a game...it all but sealed the deal. A.D. not only had an issue with his coach, but also with Isiah. It just so happens that Aguirre and Isiah are the best of friends. They also share the same agent, which becomes the basis of a conspiracy theory for Dantley. He would long blame Isiah for being traded. But also a factor was Dantley's style of play...and Isiah's. Zeke wanted to push the ball up the court. A.D. wanted to work the clock and his opponent, until he had his desired position and shot. While that was happening, movement of his teammates often came to a screeching halt. They were turned into non-participants. The ball had disappeared into a black hole....never to be seen again.

Aguirre on the other hand, loved to shoot and score. He was annually one of the leading point producers in the NBA…as he was in college. But his defense was suspect, and that was the Pistons strong suit. How was this going to work? As Isiah mentions in his book, *Bad Boys*, it started with a meeting. He met with Laimbeer, Vinnie, Mahorn, and Aguirre. Those four have the strongest personalities on the team, and they didn't mince words about who and what the Pistons are all about. Isiah basically gave Aguirre the ground rules…"No nights off. Everyone is important, has a role, and is expected to accept that role." Vinnie added…"Don't take it personal." Mahorn said, "I've got your back and you better have mine." Laimbeer in particular let it be known he was giving Aguirre a chance, in spite of all his bad press, because of Isiah. "If it weren't for Zeke," Laimbeer said, "I wouldn't even talk to you."

In the meantime, Isiah faded the heat when cornered by reporters, realizing his longtime friendship with Aguirre automatically put him in the hot seat. Dantley was extremely popular in Detroit, but when Aguirre was introduced at The Palace, he received a standing ovation…easing the tension brought on by the trade.

Aguirre learned in his first practice, a physical one, that he had to make some changes in his game and his conditioning. He was scoring over 24 points a contest for Dallas. During his time in Detroit that was cut in half. He lost weight and changed his diet, thus showing he was serious when he said, "I'm here for one reason, and that's to win a championship. I'm glad you're giving me a chance, because that's all I need."

With Aguirre on board the Pistons had all they needed, and blazed a trail through the regular season. Their 63 wins were the most in franchise history, and has only been topped by the 2005-06 team, which won 64. Their complete domination of opponents was telling in the playoffs as they swept Boston in the first round. Ditto for Milwaukee in the Eastern Conference Semifinals.

Michael Jordan and the Chicago Bulls served notice by taking two of the first three games in the Eastern Conference Finals. Jordan's pre-series prediction of the Bulls advancing to the finals, should they take game one...appeared to possibly have some validity to it. But the Pistons started displaying some of the attributes that made them successful; defense, experience, and personnel. They double-teamed Michael Jordan again ("The Jordan Rules") and Vinnie Johnson got hot in game five, as few can...with 16 points in the fourth quarter.

Scotty Pippen was literally knocked out of game six and same for the Bulls in the series, four games to two. Back to L.A. for some unfinished business.

The Pistons had been good in the playoffs, but the Lakers were perfect... sweeping Portland, Seattle, and Phoenix. However, fueled by what happened last season in the finals, and its three guard rotation of Isiah, Joe Dumars and Vinnie Johnson...playing at home, the Pistons cruised to a 109-97 victory.

Game two was uncharacteristic for the Pistons, as the Lakers were scoring at will. But Magic Johnson wouldn't finish the game due to a hamstring injury. He would join Byron Scott in the training room, who was nursing a hamstring issue of his own. Again the Pistons were led by their three guards who combined for 72 points...33 by Joe D...in a 108-105 victory.

By now it was becoming painfully (no pun intended) obvious that the Lakers, with both Magic and Byron Scott nursing hamstring injuries... were in big trouble. In addition, something else was clear, the Pistons were just too deep and talented, especially at guard, to be denied this time. The emergence of Dumars, a quiet skillful gunner from McNeese State, couldn't have come at a better time. He was the perfect complement to Isiah, allowing each to handle the point position, and when it was called for, be a scorer as well. It was Joe's time to shine...and shine he did. He followed his game two performance with 31, Isiah contributed 26, and V.J. 17. James "Big Game" Worthy and Kareem tried to pick up the slack for L.A. but to no avail, 114-110 Detroit. The Pistons were one game away from that coveted NBA crown.

Game four would be the last for arguably the greatest center to ever play the game. Kareem Abdul-Jabbar (Ferdinand Lewis Alcindor

Jr.) redefined basketball...literally. Because of his size, 7'2", and his ability to easily dunk the ball through the hoop, the shot was outlawed in 1967...not only in college, but high school as well. You couldn't even dunk in warm ups! I may not have been the highest jumper on my team at Booker T. Washington, but I could dunk and had perfected a one dribble move, starting roughly at the free throw line...that ended with a one handed jam!

I was devastated that I would never get to use it, because of Alcindor (he converted to Islam in 1968 and began using his Arabic name, Jabbar in 1971), who was in college. I couldn't understand that rule being used in high school as well.

The law against dunking lasted almost ten years. These days can you imagine basketball without the dunk? But Alcindor adapted and popularized the "Sky Hook," named because of the trajectory of the shot. From his out stretched right hand...the ball took a downward path into the basket. He shot it so fluidly. His foot work, and the rotation of his body, would have made Fred Astaire envious. It was basically an unstoppable shot. But after game four, Kareem and his "Sky Hook" would become part of basketball history.

It was the Bad Boys' long awaited moment and they too were headed into "round ball" annals! Worthy played up to his "Big Game" name by scoring 40 points, but no one else contributed more than 13. The Lakers are swept away 105-97. Dumars scored 23 to lead the team and is named Most Valuable Player in the Finals. THE PISTONS ARE CHAMPS!

Let the celebrating begin, but it wouldn't last long. In what has to be the cruelest timing inflicted on any team, two days after clinching the NBA title...just after the parade and during a ceremony at The Palace, comes news that Rick Mahorn has been selected by Minnesota in the NBA expansion draft.

The Pistons rotated nine players...Isiah, Dumars, Laimbeer, Aguirre, Rodman, Salley, Vinnie Johnson, James Edwards, and Mahorn...but they could only protect eight. The team didn't want to part with V.J.

despite his age and a new contract. He was the "Microwave", instant points off the bench...the best six man in the game. James "Buddha" Edwards was a 7-foot low post force. That left Mahorn, a team leader and who's physical play discouraged opponents...the odd man out. Officials were quick to call a foul on him, and he wasn't playing much because of that and a bad back.

The Pistons thought maybe they could offer a draft pick in exchange...should Mahorn be selected, but that wasn't appealing to Minnesota who took him and later traded him to Philadelphia. Mahorn would return to Detroit during the 1996-98 seasons, after stops in Italy and New Jersey.

Twice as Nice

That banging on the door of the Pistons was not room service, more like a wake-up call. Michael Jordan and the Chicago Bulls had taken their lumps and were eager to enjoy some championship champagne. Sure the Pistons were defending NBA champs, had finished on top of the Eastern Division and with a 72% winning percentage. However, anyone who follows pro basketball knows that the real season starts in the playoffs. After breezing past Indiana and New York, the 1989-90 campaign was about to be elevated to new heights and many fans felt Michael Jordan would be in the starring role as Superman.

True to his marquee billing, Jordan was magnificent and the Bulls, after losing the first two games, bounced back with two wins of their own. This back and forth scenario would boil down to a game seven at The Palace. Winner take all.

As it turns out the Pistons had little to worry about...because even Superman needs rest every now and then, at least this one does. Detroit rolls into its third consecutive NBA finals by dispatching M.J. and the Bulls 93-74.

My mind drifted back to a couple of years ago in Los Angeles, and that phantom foul called on Laimbeer, that sent Kareem to the free throw line. Minus those two foul shots the Pistons could be on the verge of celebrating their third straight championship. Make no mistake... Portland, which eliminated Phoenix four games to two, in the Western Conference finals, had some players. Clyde "The Glide" Drexler, Terry Porter, Buck Williams, Jerome Kersey, and Kevin Duckworth were not to be overlooked. In addition, the Pistons had lost 17 straight in Portland. But this was a matchup I felt favored Detroit.

The teams would split the opening two games at The Palace, as the well-rested Trailblazers stole an overtime thriller, 106-105 in game two. Game three started on a somber note when it was learned Joe Dumars' father had passed following complications with severe diabetes. Joe D.'s wife Debbie, pleaded with Chuck Daly not to give Joe D. the news until after the game. In addition, Dennis Rodman, who had been battling an ankle injury, wouldn't play. After learning of his father's death following the contest, Dumars said this explained the way he played that night, and figured his dad had something to do with it. He scored 33 in a 121-106 blowout by the Pistons.

A hot hand by Isiah propelled the Pistons to a 112-109 victory in game four. Zeke had 32. The Pistons were one win away from another title and thanks to "The Microwave," it soon became a reality. V.J. also picked up a new nickname, because with 00.07 left on the clock, his 15-foot jumper over Jerome Kersey sealed the deal. The Pistons celebrate their second consecutive championship thanks to a 92-90 victory. Isiah is named MVP of the finals by averaging over 27 points during the five game series. Time for another parade!

When the Tigers won it all in 1984 I wondered to myself, is this all there is? No more games? But in the case of the Pistons and their two straight titles, it had been a long climb to the top. Everyone connected with the team, and covering it, seemed to be feeling exhausted. I realized becoming champ, especially on a professional level, is not only exhausting physically, but mentally as well. There is no time off while you're in the hunt or being hunted. It magnifies the accomplishments of the great dynasties that find a way, and will to challenge... year in and year out.

Flying High with the Wings

This turns my thoughts and memories to the Detroit Red Wings. During my tenure at Channel 7, their raucous, rowdy rise to the top of the National Hockey League contains recollections that could fill the rest of this book. From Head Coaches Nick Polano to Dave Lewis and General Managers Jimmy Devellano to Ken Holland, there were talented and driven rosters sprinkled with mystique, intrigue, and players from all around the globe. In addition, the organization also enjoyed two incredible, irreplaceable people...owner Mike Ilitch Sr. and Captain Steve Yzerman.

When Mr. "I" purchased the Red Wings in June of 1982, the team had missed the playoffs 14 out of 16 seasons. Stevie "Y" was selected in the 1983 NHL draft and at the age of 21, was named captain in '86, becoming the youngest ever to wear the "C" on his jersey. Over the next 19 years, the Red Wings would miss the playoffs only once, while capturing three Stanley Cups. In the process they would turn Motown into HockeyTown.

But like the Pistons this was no overnight success story...hardly. During many a pre-game skate in Joe Louis Arena, the Wings could only sit and watch Wayne Gretzky and the talented Edmonton Oilers put on skating exhibitions, highlighted by dazzling passes...and realize they were beaten before the first puck could hit the ice that night.

The home team would fight back, literally, with the notorious "Bruise Brothers", Bob Probert and Joey Kocur, inflicting punishment on opponents, thus giving hungry fans something to cheer about... when what they really wanted were wins.

A young Petr Klima defected from Czechoslovakia to help with some of the offensive deficiencies. He had a flowing mullet and easy smile, but also some issues with partying and alcohol, which kept him from reaching his full potential. He and Bob Probert would even room together for a while, making for a sometimes toxic mix that caused major problems for the team. By the late 80's Probert's drinking and addiction to cocaine would lead to a six month prison term.

Fortunately Steve Yzerman was enjoying the kind of offensive production that kept "The Joe" buzzing. During the '88-'89 season, his 65 goals and 90 assists placed him third in NHL scoring behind Mario Lemieux and Wayne Gretzky. Yzerman captured Most Valuable Player honors, as voted by the National Hockey League Players' Association.

The team was becoming a regular in the playoffs, but the much sought after championships were still years away. Jacques Demers had become a fan favorite behind the bench, and the majority of us covering the team also enjoyed the passionate and emotional Canadian. He had brought the Wings back to life, but after missing the post season in 1989-90, Demers was fired. He got some redemption a few years later when he captured the Stanley Cup with Montreal in 1992-93.

However, the most amazing thing about Demers was that he was functionally illiterate. He claimed he never learned to read or write because of his abusive childhood in Montreal. Demers said he covered for himself by having secretaries and public relations personnel read letters for him. They thought he couldn't read English well enough to understand the correspondence. This pretense continued until release of his biography in 2005. I, like so many others, never had a clue of what he was going through...unbelievable!

LEARNING TO SPEAK RUSSIAN

Adapt or become history. I'm sure some famous person said it first, but in life and in particular sports, never a truer statement has been made, which brings us to Sergei Fedorov and an entirely different look for the Red Wings. But first a little intrigue; after being drafted in 1989, but while still playing for Russia, Fedorov defects during an exhibition in Portland, Oregon.

He gets kicked out of the game for fighting (Sergei fighting, really?). He changes into street clothes and watches the remainder of the contest with his teammates. However, at the end of the game, he quietly slips into the crowd, blends in and eventually boards a plane for Detroit...with assists going to Red Wings Vice President Jim Lites and former head coach Nick Polano, among others. I give Fedorov credit, he was as slick off the ice...as he was on it.

He was described as being three players in one because of his offensive and defensive skills, and was talked about in glowing terms by both Gretzky and Yzerman, a couple of former league MVPs, a list Fedorov would soon join.

Personally, I just liked the guy. His skills were obvious, but the way he connected with those of us in the media showed talents I honestly didn't expect. But what was I supposed to make of a Russian hockey player? I don't think that's a question that ever crossed my mind.

What Fedorov helped me realize was that Russians, Canadians, Czechs, Swedes...even Americans, are all basically alike...with many of the same goals and hopes, especially where team and family are concerned. He was an amazing, amazing player, but just as Yzerman learned, you need all the help you can get to hoist that Stanley Cup.

Bryan Murray "righted the ship" and once again had the team in the playoffs, only to fall short of the desired NHL championship. Enter Scotty Bowman in 1993, arguably one of the greatest coaches in history...in any sport. When he joined the Red Wings, Bowman had already won five Stanley Cups with the Montreal Canadiens, so nothing less was expected in Detroit. Bowman's approach to the game and his style often clashed with his players, including his Captain Steve Yzerman.

I can tell you from personal experience that Bowman could be a challenge to deal with. I remember one trip to Denver in which I was supposed to supply post-game coverage back to Detroit. The Red Wings and Avalanche had turned into a heated rivalry, anything could happen. I couldn't relax until the broadcast was over.

It was a hotly contested game, as expected, won by the Red Wings. I had submitted my plans and received approval from the team for interviews, plus I was the only Detroit TV reporter...which meant requests were at a minimum. It didn't matter to Bowman, who wanted to get to the airport as soon as possible. The crew I picked up in Denver wondered out loud if I was working for the Avalanche because of the way I was being treated. It was Bowman being Bowman. He was the man in charge…of everything. But the end results were all that mattered, let's go! I had to get in line with everyone else, and scrambled for whatever I could get.

By 1995 Scotty Bowman and the Red Wings would finally reach the Stanley Cup Finals. The Russian Five were on board and creating major problems for opponents. Vyacheslav "Slava" Kozlov, Igor "The Professor" Larionov, Viacheslav Fetisov, Vladimir Konstantinov, and Sergei Fedorov were all legends in their native Russia.

Their displays of speed and puck control were something to see. They helped keep Joe Louis Arena buzzing and Zamboni driver Al Sobotka busy, cleaning up all the octopi that were flying onto the ice (a tradition dating back to the 1952 playoffs. The eight arms of the octopus represented the number of playoff wins then, that it would take to capture the Stanley Cup. The Metro Times newspaper reported that 35 of the slimy suckers littered "The Joe's" frozen pond during the final home game in 2017).

The roster also included Nick Lidstrom and Paul Coffey, two of the best defenseman in NHL history, the "Grind Line" of Darren McCarty, Kris Draper, and Kirk Maltby, sniper Dino Ciccarelli, another of the seven Red Wings who would end up in the Hall Of Fame, along with Stevie "Y"…and a couple of capable goalies, Chris Osgood and Mike Vernon.

A prolonged labor dispute between the owners and the Players Association delayed the start of the regular season. The impasse lasted into the next year and an abbreviated season of 48 games was played. The Red Wings breezed through the competition, picking up the Central Division and Western Conference titles…and the Presidents' Trophy for having the best record in the league.

They dominated Dallas four to one in the opening round of the playoffs, outscored San Jose 24-6 in four straight, and eliminated Chicago in the Western Conference Finals, four-games to one. But in the Stanley Cup Finals, the Wings first appearance since 1966, their offense was brought to a screeching halt thanks to New Jersey's neutral-zone trap defense. It held the high flying Red Wings to just seven goals, during a sweep for the Devils.

Hockey's Hatfields and McCoys

I had to give the devil its due (pun most definitely intended). Not much to be said when you're broomed out of a competition. Who saw that coming? But excitement we could have never imagined was about to ignite the hockey world, and all of sports for that matter.

There must be something in Detroiters' blood, a kind of resilient blue collar grit, possibly forged in the auto plants that dot the local landscape. How else do you explain the Pistons, Red Wings and Tigers having that swagger...and the "us against the world" chip on their shoulders? Come to think of it, it's in the restaurants, barber shops, salons, churches, schools, and dentist offices throughout the neighborhoods.

So when the 1995-96 year materialized, the Wings were ready again. They set a record for regular season wins (62), and fell just two points shy of surpassing the mark for points. Again, they captured the Presidents' Trophy...but again the Stanley Cup eluded them as they fell to the Colorado Avalanche, the eventual champion, four games to two, in the Western Conference Finals. During the first period of the final game, Colorado's Claude Lemieux lived up to his reputation for being one of the dirtiest players in the league.

Lemieux hit Kris Draper from behind, sending him into the boards face first. The popular Draper suffered a concussion, broken jaw, broken nose, and broken cheekbone...all of which led him to having reconstructive surgery on his face and his jaw being wired shut for several weeks. Thus, one of the most competitive rivalries in sports was born. To add insult to Draper's injuries, Lemieux was a nemesis during the embarrassing sweep by New Jersey the previous year.

Draper would return to the ice and was even named alternate captain of the Red Wings, before retiring in the spring of 2011. He is one of only seven players to wear the uniform for at least one thousand games. One of his most exciting and thrilling contests featured payback for Draper, with a little help from his friends. It became known as "Brawl in HockeyTown." The two teams had met three times since Draper was injured, but March 26, 1997, was the first visit to Detroit by Lemieux since his attack on Draper. On this night, a sold out crowd at Joe Louis Arena was treated to ten fights, one even involved the goalies, Mike Vernon and Patrick Roy.

Darren McCarty, Draper's linemate, saw Lemieux watching Igor Larionov and Peter Forsberg tussle and sent a fist to the temple of the distracted Lemieux. The next thing he knew he was on his back. Lemieux managed to get to his knees and tried to cover up in a turtle position, as McCarty pounded him with left hands. Bodies and fists were flying and the crowd cheered every blow. Lemieux's face was a bloody mess as he left the ice. McCarty's night became even better when he tipped in the game winner in overtime. The 6 to 5, come from behind win, and the fights seemed to energize a Wings team that hadn't shown its usual dominance during the regular season.

They would carry the momentum into the playoffs and with goalie Mike Vernon enjoying MVP performances...eliminate St. Louis four games to two, sweep Anaheim, beat Colorado four to two in the Conference finals, and hold Philadelphia winless in the Stanley Cup Finals.

After a 42 year wait...THEY FINALLY DRINK FROM THE CUP! Time to celebrate. First, a party at Joe Louis Arena for the season ticket holders...and the following day, a parade down Woodward with a million or so well wishers lining the street, all the way to Hart plaza. It was quite a sight.

Three days later, Friday June 13th around 10pm, I'm finishing up what has been a long day, and anxiously looking forward to tomorrow...and a vacation. The assignment editor calls and tells me...as soon as I finish the 11:00 sports, I need to run over to Beaumont Hospital.

Members of the Red Wings have been involved in an automobile accident. It's a serious one. I need to help identify the people coming and going, then be ready for a live shot as soon as we are set up. I start making phone calls to get additional information. My mind is racing. How could this happen? Six days ago the whole town was jubilant, now this. How many are involved? How seriously are they injured?

The somber faces arriving at Beaumont relayed the seriousness of the situation. Vladimir Konstantinov, Viacheslav Fetisov, two of the Russian Five, team masseur Sergei Mnatsakaniov and limo driver Richard Gnida, hit a tree. Apparently Gnida had fallen asleep. The impact, while not fatal, had done some serious damage, particularly to Konstantinov and Mnatsakaniov. They would never be the same.

THE IRONY OF FATE

Konstantinov, the 30-year-old hard charging defenseman, was establishing himself as one of the best to ever play in the NHL. The Hall of Fame was a definite possibility when he retired. He was diagnosed with what doctors called a scrambled brain. Like the others, Vladimir wasn't wearing a seat belt and was left in a coma for weeks. Twenty years after the accident he was living with full-time caretakers, in need of a walker to get around and had not regained full mobility or mental faculties. His wife, Irina, had moved to Florida.

Sergei Mnatsakanov, the team masseur, was paralyzed from the waist down, in a coma and faced the most immediate struggle for survival.

Slava Fetisov, who was instrumental in helping Soviet players join the National Hockey League, escaped with minor injuries and was able to continue his playing career. Ironically, 12 years prior to this crash, Fetisov was also involved in an automobile accident that killed a younger brother.

Richard Gnida, the Red Wings limousine driver, walked away without significant injuries. He was driving with a suspended license that had been revoked the year before. In addition, Gnida had numerous traffic violations in his past, including speeding and driving under the influence. A judge sentenced him to nine months in jail and ordered him to perform 200 hours of community service at a facility for patients with head injuries. The jail term was followed by 15 months of probation. It was his second conviction for driving with a suspended license.

The Red Wings would also win the Stanley Cup the following year in 1998, again in 2002 and 2008. They qualified for the playoffs 25 consecutive years until 2017. A remarkable achievement but many faithful wonder, had the crash not happened, how much more success the team and Konstantinov would have enjoyed. We will never know.

CHAPTER 9

Wanted – A Michigan Man!

M-23 TO INTERSTATE 96 MAY be the popular route….or maybe it's the reverse. Depends on your destination I guess, the University of Michigan or Michigan State University? It is most definitely a one or the other choice, right down to the press room menu on game day. Is this farm to table (MSU)? Or delectable (hot) dogs (U of M)? Being an Okie by birth, it doesn't really matter. You see, thanks to my daughters' college choices…I'm invested in both schools.

The rivalry didn't figure in my decision to move from Chi-town to Mo-town, however from a professional perspective, I couldn't be happier. From football to field hockey…and from basketball to baseball, there is always something going on supplying thousands of opportunities for Spartans and Wolverines to claim, "We're number one and you're not!" The fact that both universities are in the Big Ten Conference only amps up the volume.

It's fitting I guess, that both schools captured Men's NCAA Basketball Championships during my tenure at WXYZ, but the way Michigan did it, could never have been predicted; by firing Head Coach Bill Frieder just two days before the tournament started! Who does that? The "Bodacious One" (which is what I fondly called him, but not to his face!) AKA Bo Schembechler, Michigan head football coach and athletic director, that's who.

Frieder was quoted in the *New York Times* as saying, he was offered the Arizona State job three years prior and was pressured into making a decision before the NCAA Tournament. On Selection Sunday, he announced his decision with the intention of coaching his team through the 1989 tournament. He said he had become disenchanted with the direction of the program under Schembechler. Frieder pointed to the cutting of chartered flights and trimming recruiting perks as some of his issues with Michigan. He admitted the timing of his announcement could have been handled differently. But Frieder said he wanted to be upfront and honest.

That's when Bo made his famous statement…"I don't want someone from Arizona State coaching the Michigan team, a Michigan man is going to coach Michigan." Schembechler then elevated Steve Fisher, Frieder's longtime friend and Michigan assistant coach, to the position of interim head coach. Oddly, Frieder's pedigree is that of a Michigan man and not Fisher's. Frieder grew up in Saginaw, coached Flint Northern High School to back to back Class A state titles, and was a U-M grad, class of 1964. Fisher grew up in Illinois and played for Illinois State, before becoming an assistant at Michigan in 1982. But Bo's Michigan man statement was clear, and followed him for the remainder of his life.

Spurred on because of, or in spite of, the controversy…10th ranked Michigan, after a third place finish in the Big Ten Conference, entered the NCAA tournament looking for its first national championship in school history.

COOKING WITH RICE

The team ran hot and cold during the regular season, ranked as high as #2 in the country and as low as #13. But it was coming into the tournament following an embarrassing 16 point loss to fourth ranked Illinois at Crisler Arena. Add the Frieder fiasco and a national title didn't seem attainable; how about just surviving? But the Wolverines weren't short on confidence or talent. Leading the way was a hot-shot out of Flint Northwestern High School named Glen Rice. Long, lean with a jumper...that was mean, or as he would later be identified, "G-Money." The G stood for guaranteed (to go in).

Rice could stroke it from downtown, slam it, and at 6'8" a matchup nightmare for the opposition. His record setting performances assured Michigan of at least a chance to win. Rumeal Robinson, Loy Vaught, Terry Mills and Sean Higgins all averaged in double figures. Mark Hughes led an able bench. Fisher knew his players' capabilities, but he also knew this was an unusual situation...one that he had never encountered; he turned to Bo.

As was detailed in his book, "Bo's Lasting Lessons," co-authored by John U. Bacon, Schembechler met with the team and complimented each player until he got to Sean Higgins. Higgins was from Ann Arbor and had been quoted in the Ann Arbor News that he would transfer if he didn't like the new coach. Bo told Higgins he has his transfer papers upstairs on his desk and the transaction could be done by lunch. Higgins admitted he was caught off guard and wasn't about to leave. Higgins said the encounter was different from what the players were used to and it fired the team up, coming from someone they all respected. Schembechler was with them every step they took toward the title, making sure they didn't have to face the media alone.

Odds of Fisher remaining the head coach after the tournament were slim at best. Speculation of who would succeed him was a daily activity. Fisher said he didn't weigh a lot to begin with, but lost 10 to15 pounds during the tournament. He could breathe a little easier after an opening round win over Xavier, 92-87. Fisher's fans grew, but it appeared Schembechler wasn't one of them. He reportedly didn't like some of the people associating with the program under Frieder and wanted to go in another direction by hiring someone from the outside.

Michigan eliminated South Alabama 91-82 to move into the Sweet Sixteen. Then it knocked off fifth Ranked North Carolina 92-87 and Virginia 102-65 in the Elite Eight, to advance to the Final Four against Conference foe Illinois. The same team that sent Michigan into the tournament reeling from a 16-point defeat. It was the speed of Illinois against the size of Michigan. Rice continued to enjoy an outstanding season, even increasing his scoring production that led the Big Ten Conference. Rumeal's ball handling and the rebounding of Loy Vaught helped Michigan prevail. However, this see-saw contest wasn't decided until Higgins scored on a put back with two seconds remaining…sealing the Wolverines' 83-81 win, which sent them into the championship game against Seton Hall.

Unlikely and improbable Michigan would need one more night of magic, and it would get it. But not before John Morton's three-pointer sends it into overtime for Seton Hall, tied at 71. It was one of those classic…I can't watch, but I can't stop watching thrillers! The Wolverines are down 79-76, when Terry Mills turns and scores. Michigan is within one…56 ticks left. John Morton, who led all scorers with 35, can't hit inside the lane, 13 seconds remain.

Rice rebounds to Rumeal, who without hesitation, takes it the length of the court. He spots Mark Hughes to his right, but is fouled by Seton Hall's Gerald Greene while attempting to pass …three seconds left. The Pirates were outraged. I can't blame them, it was a ticky-tack call. For the season Rumeal was averaging only 65% from the line. But on this night he hit nine of ten free throws, including the two that delivered the national championship to Ann Arbor…and wiped "interim" away from Steve Fisher's title.

Sunshine…Followed by Storms

> "Can it be that it was all so simple then? Or has time re-written every line? If we had the chance to do it all again…Tell me, would we? Could we?"

When I reflect back on what followed Michigan's national championship, I can't get the lyrics of "The Way We Were" out of my mind. That classic song, written by Marvin Hamlisch and Alan and Marilyn

Bergman, might seem a little melodramatic to some, considering the Wolverines' wounds were mostly self-inflicted...but there were also innocent victims who suffered needlessly.

> "Memories...may be beautiful and yet, what's too painful to remember, we simply choose to forget."

Prominence and prestige followed Michigan back to Ann Arbor, along with that oversized trophy. The school became a hot spot for talented basketball players...too hot! Envious opponents often are the first to recognize it and also as the saying goes..."loose lips, sink ships." Within a couple of years, Steve Fisher had what many thought was the most talented class of freshmen ever assembled on one team. Chris Webber, Juwan Howard, Jalen Rose, Ray Jackson, and Jimmy King became known as the "Fab Five." Like the Beatles, they created quite a stir...with their baggy shorts, black socks, and defiant swagger.

Chris Webber, the most well-known of the quintet, hit the radar of round-ball followers as a 6'5" middle schooler. He became an annual visit for me and my crew, to chronicle his progress and see how much he had grown physically. This continued throughout high school, where he and his Detroit Country Day teammates captured three state championships.

Over at Detroit Southwestern High School, Jalen Rose was creating a name for himself, along with some other future NBA standouts. Under the guidance of legendary Head Coach Perry Watson, who later become an assistant coach at the University of Michigan, the Prospectors were annually in the hunt for a state title.

Meanwhile, Juwan Howard was becoming a McDonald's All-America at Chicago's Vocational High School. At 6'9", he was the perfect complement to the 6'10 Webber and Rose, who stood 6'8".

6'6" Ray Jackson rattled rims with thunderous dunks at LBJ High School in Austin, Texas, and caught Michigan's eye. In Plano, Texas... just outside of Dallas, 6'5" All-America guard Jimmy King, was also a must-have for the Wolverines.

Immediately after arriving on campus, the Fab Five declared they would shock the world and set out to do just that.

December 14th, 1991, I'm in New York City covering The Heisman Trophy presentation that honored Desmond Howard, U of M's outstanding receiver and kick returner. Many of the reporters, waiting for the proceedings to begin, were gathered around a television and not believing what they were seeing. The broadcast was coming from Crisler Arena on the Michigan Campus, and it had nothing to do with Desmond or football.

Those highly recruited and much talked about freshman basketball players were in the process of doing just what they had predicted... shocking the world. Top- ranked Duke, led by future Pistons star Grant Hill, was in a fight that would turn into an overtime thriller. In fact, it was the Blue Devils, who had to claw their way back to send it into O.T., thanks to a trio of free throws by Bobby Hurley. This was only the fifth game of the season! Duke would prevail 88-85 but Michigan's youngsters, three of whom were starters (Webber, Rose, Howard) had served notice...as good as advertised. Michigan had out shot and out rebounded the defending NCAA champs...but were outscored 31-14 at the free throw line.

That game suggested anything could be possible this year. However, Michigan would only finish third in the Big Ten Conference, behind Ohio State and Indiana...and tied with Michigan State. The 1992 NCAA Tournament allowed another opportunity for Michigan to stun college basketball, and it came close.

In succession...Temple, East Tennessee State, and Oklahoma State fell. Then came a rematch with third ranked Ohio State and Jimmy Jackson in the Elite Eight and revenge; as Michigan won 75-71 in overtime, after being swept by the Buckeyes during the regular season.

In the Final Four, Michigan beat Cincinnati 76-72, setting up another showdown against Duke, this time for the national championship. Sadly for fans of the Wolverines, it wasn't close. Duke connected on its final twelve possessions to break it open, outscoring Michigan

41-20 in the second half, while posting a 71-51 victory, en route to its second consecutive national title.

The 1992-93 regular season featured an early match with Duke at Cameron Indoor Stadium, in Durham, North Carolina. The results were similar to the previous two games, this time a 79-68 victory for the Blue Devils. Michigan would follow that loss with eleven straight victories, and then end its Big Ten campaign with a seven game winning streak.

Top ranked Indiana was the conference champ, Michigan second. The Wolverines headed to another NCAA Tournament, this time as the top seed in the West Regional. Chris Webber had replaced Jalen Rose as the leading scorer, averaging 19.2 points a game and 10.1 rebounds. Rose 15.4, Juwan Howard 14.6, and Jimmy King 10.8, also averaged in double figures.

Michigan opened the tourney by beating Coastal Carolina by 29. The next game against UCLA came down to the final 9.6 seconds in overtime. Bruins' fans know the outcome never should have happened. UCLA had a 19-point advantage, 49-30, with 2:37 remaining in the first half, only to watch the lead evaporate as Michigan came charging back. The game went into overtime tied at 77. Fast forward... it's Michigan's ball, seven seconds on the shot clock, nine-point-six on the game clock...game is tied at 84.

Following a Michigan timeout, Jalen Rose misses his shot, but King is there for the put-back. Bruins' Head Coach, Jim Harrick argued that the shot clock had expired before Rose's shot hit the rim. Therefore the game is still tied and King's basket should not count. The zebras would huddle...instant replay agrees with the Wolverines. One-point-five seconds remain, UCLA's last second desperation attempt is off the mark. Michigan advances 86-84, in a tournament littered with upsets.

George Washington would lose to the Wolverines, as well as Temple. It sets up a confrontation with second-ranked Kentucky and Jamal Mashburn, in a Louisiana Superdome Final Four. Again, Webber leads the way with 27 points and 13 rebounds, in a physical 81-78 win for Michigan. It sends the Wolverines to their second consecutive NCAA Championship game, this time against North Carolina.

Anyone have a clue about what happens next? If you do, raise your hand. Of course I can't see you, just checking to see if you're paying attention.

Chris Webber will forever have that infamous timeout call linked to him. As a former athlete; I not only feel for Chris, but how about Bill Buckner and every competitor who has been in that position, when something goes terribly wrong and you can't take a mulligan, like in golf...and have an opportunity to do it again.

When watching Jeopardy or Wheel of Fortune I often remind my wife that "under the lights" crazy things can happen and you can't take 'em back. Same goes when you're delivering the 6:00 news. It's live, and once you've said it...that's it, good or bad.

One example is the 1986 World Series, Boston against the heavily favored New York Mets. Game six, bottom of the 10th inning. Buckner rushes a grounder off the bat of Mookie Wilson. It rolls through his legs and into right field, allowing Ray Knight to score the winning run from second base. It sends the series, tied at three, to a game seven. Boston led it three to nothing in the sixth, but the Mets scored three in the inning and three more in the seventh, eventually winning 8-5 for their second World Series Championship in franchise history. Buckner would get two hits in four appearances at the plate. He also scored a run. Yet he becomes the scapegoat and blamed for Boston losing the series. Buckner would receive death threats, he was heckled, even booed by his own fans.

I covered Buckner when he played for the Chicago Cubs. He was the epitome of class. Despite injuries to his legs and ankles, "Billy Buck" hit over .300 four times for the downtrodden Cubs. He led the National League with a .324 batting average in 1980. Human error, as the great humble Howard Cosell used to say, is why we play the games. You can't look at a lineup on paper and predict the outcome. It's why the underdog, or the backup quarterback is so beloved!

In the case of Chris Webber and Michigan…their swagger, baggie shorts, and black socks placed them firmly in the "bad guys" role. Can't have a good guy, without a villain…right? 20 seconds left in the championship game against North Carolina. Michigan trails by two with no timeouts. That was established and confirmed during Michigan's final huddle. Michigan guard Dugan Fife said, "It was so loud in the arena, that you couldn't hear yourself think."

Webber rebounds a missed free throw by the Tar Heels. He thought about passing to Jalen Rose and in the process travels, but the refs don't call it. He then dribbles into the corner, near the Michigan bench, right into North Carolina's trap and is double teamed. Webber then turns and signals for a timeout. He said he heard someone scream timeout from the Michigan bench. Calling a timeout when you don't have one is a technical foul. Two free throws for North Carolina and it will get the ball. Tar Heels hit both free throws and add two more when Michigan is forced to intentionally foul. Game over! 77-71 North Carolina…the new NCAA Champion.

The 1993 NBA draft was held at The Palace of Auburn Hills, just outside of Detroit. Chris Webber didn't have far to travel when he was drafted first overall by the Orlando Magic, making him also the first member of the Fab Five to leave school. Juwan Howard (Washington Bullets, fifth pick) and Jalen Rose (Denver Nuggets, 13th pick) would follow in 1994. Jimmy King was selected by the Toronto Raptors in the second round of the 1995 draft. Ray Jackson was not drafted, nor did he compete in the NBA, but he did play for the Grand Rapids Hoops in the Continental Basketball Association.

The Fab Five arrived in Ann Arbor expecting to shock the world, but had to be stunned themselves…leaving and not even winning a Big Ten Title. What success they did have, including a 31 win season in 1992-93, would be wiped from the record books because of a scandal involving Chris Webber, future Wolverines' Maurice Taylor, Robert "Tractor" Traylor, Louis Bullock, and a retired auto worker named Ed Martin.

In an attempt at full disclosure, and as I pointed out earlier in this book, I was ready to leave the University of Wyoming after my first semester as a freshman, because of its lack of Black female co-eds and a social life, among other things. But a sympathetic assistant football coach told me that if my soon-to-be wife had qualifying grades, and she did...that she could become a student and join me at the university. She was there by the beginning of January.

To the best of my understanding, money in the general university fund enabled this to happen. In addition, I was told the fund would also be used to recruit other African-American females, because of the university's deficient numbers. Was this legal? I wasn't about to "look a gift horse in the mouth" and was very grateful.

In the late 60's, we were limited to receiving just $15 a month as an allowance, presumably to do our laundry. I'm not sure if...or how much that has changed. But the explosion of money involved in intercollegiate athletics: television contracts, the amount distributed for basketball tournament appearances, payouts for bowl games, coaches' salaries, and the increasing number of manufacturers connected with the schools can't help but create problems...and it has, big time.

I certainly don't have all the answers, but those who are profiting the most "above board" should spread around more of the wealth. It only makes sense, but the National Collegiate Athletic Association (NCAA) hasn't figured it out, or doesn't want to share with the athletes in a more equitable fashion. Would this stop the illegal activities involved in the "amateur" sports? I'm not that naïve, but the way things are now is not working...and destined only to get worse.

It is presumed Ed Martin was one of the people Schembechler expressed concerns about during the firing of Bill Frieder, before he officially hired Steve Fisher as head coach. Two years after the Fab Five left the University of Michigan, it was learned Martin, a person who had befriended Jalen Rose and a number of high school players, received a visit from Maurice Taylor.

Taylor, Big Ten Freshman of the Year, and second Team All-Big Ten as a sophomore, was involved in an automobile accident, along with

Robert Traylor, apparently after leaving Ed Martin's home. They were reportedly helping recruit Mateen Cleaves, a future Michigan State star. Traylor suffered a broken arm in the accident, and it led to an investigation by both Michigan and the Big Ten Conference. It was learned that Fisher had arranged for complimentary tickets for Martin. Fisher was fired and Martin was banned from the program.

During a news conference about the growing scandal, I asked if Assistant Coach Perry Watson had been found guilty of doing anything wrong. There had been much speculation about Watson's possible role in this mess. The former longtime head coach at Detroit Southwestern appeared guilty by association. No one had come to his defense, until I asked the question. He at last was exonerated.

In 2002, Ed Martin was indicted in federal court, charged with running an illegal gambling operation and money laundering. The indictment also claimed that Martin gave Chris Webber $280,000 in illicit loans while he starred in high school and college, with another $360,000 allegedly going to former Wolverines' Taylor, Robert "Tractor" Traylor, and Louis Bullock. Martin originally denied that he had ever given money to players while they were at Michigan. But following some much publicized FBI raids on a number of homes, one belonging to Martin, he eventually testified that he paid Webber, Traylor, Taylor and Bullock $616,000.

Webber, who denied taking money while at Michigan, was indicted on charges of obstruction of justice, and lying to a grand jury. He vowed to fight the charges. However, Webber later avoided jail time by entering a guilty plea to a lesser charge of criminal contempt. He admitted to lying before a grand jury, and claimed he received over $38,000 from Martin, who passed away in 2003, while waiting to be sentenced.

THE AFTERMATH IN ANN ARBOR

In November 2002, Michigan announces self-sanctions on the men's basketball program. The University vacates the Fab Five's second season, 1992-93, including every statistic. In addition, President Mary Sue

Coleman includes the Wolverines' Final Four appearance in 1992; it never happened. The 1992 and 1993 Final Four banners are removed from Crisler Arena. The NCAA delivered its own penalties as well. It forced the University of Michigan to disassociate itself from Traylor, Bullock, and Taylor until 2012 and Webber until 2013. Michigan also lost scholarships. A post-season ban was imposed in 2002-2003.

I received a call from Jalen Rose's mom who was furious, complaining that innocent players, including her son Jalen, shouldn't be penalized! I interviewed her, and agreed that players who had nothing to do with this scandal are probably being wrongly implicated, and shouldn't have to suffer.

But according to the rigid and ridiculous rules of the NCAA, when even accepting a free meal can constitute a violation, who can really, truthfully be considered clean? This example may sound extreme, but under certain circumstances that hamburger could become a problem.

Apparently politicians in California and North Carolina feel the same way and are putting pressure on the NCAA to permit college athletes to be paid in certain situations. But during the Summer of 2019, the NCAA was threatening to fight back, even insinuating, regarding a California bill, "Fair Pay to Play Act," it would bar institutions in that state from participating in NCAA's championships if the bill passes. The NCAA says it wants to study its position on compensation for athletes and deliver a final report on the subject in October of 2019.

Chris Webber and Jalen Rose had issues of their own…with each other. According to his book, "Give the People What They Want," Rose says he asked Webber to distance himself from Ed Martin, but he didn't, and should apologize. Rose feels that relationship was the downfall of their time in Ann Arbor. An ESPN documentary on the Fab Five, produced by Rose, didn't help their situation. Webber claims he wasn't contacted about participating until the last minute, which was disputed by Rose and Jimmy King. Webber was the only Fab Five member not in the program.

Rose, who has reconnected with the Michigan basketball program, is also trying to have the banners returned to the rafters in Crisler

Arena. In addition, Rose thinks Steve Fisher should receive Hall of Fame consideration, but is not getting it because of the Martin scandal. Fisher, after being fired at U of M, eventually landed at San Diego State, where he was head coach for 18 years. He compiled a record of 386 wins and 209 losses, before retiring after the 2016-2017 season.

Perry Watson left Michigan after the 1993 season. He became head coach at the University of Detroit, where he enjoyed a Hall of Fame Career over the next 15 years.

In May of 2019, a tearful Juwan Howard replaced John Beilein as Michigan's head basketball coach.

"Those Who Stay will be Champions"

1995 was Lloyd Carr's first year as Michigan's head football coach. He was a longtime assistant under Bo Schembechler, eventually becoming the Wolverines' defensive coordinator, and assistant head coach. I liked Carr mainly because of his similarities to Bo. He lived and breathed Michigan with plenty of fire, if the occasion called for it. Carr showed genuine concern for his players, and while careful when dealing with us reporter types, he could still flash that infectious smile, and joke with us while being interviewed. So even though the discussion may have been serious at times, his style and explanations made my job less difficult. I appreciated that.

After a couple of average years (for Michigan's expectations), with a record of nine and four in 1995 and eight and four in '96, and with both seasons ending in bowl game losses, 1997 wasn't expected to turn out the way it did. The pre-season Coaches' Poll had Michigan ranked 17[th,] and facing a very tough schedule. First, Carr had to decide who would quarterback the team. Brian Griese, a fifth year senior, got the nod over Tom Brady.

The defense, led by cornerback Charles Woodson, an eventual Heisman Trophy winner, ended up being one of the best in Michigan history. Defensive ends Glen Steele and James Hall, along with linebackers Dhani Jones, Sam Sword, and Ian Gold made life difficult for opponents. Strong safety Marcus Ray was also a force.

Joining Griese on offense was a line that included Jeff Backus, Steve Hutchinson, and Jon Janson. Tight ends Jerame Tuman and Aaron Shea were reliable, as were wide receivers Tai Streets, Russell Shaw, and Woodson. Chris Howard, Anthony Thomas, and Clarence Williams were also targets out of the backfield. Howard was the leading rusher, with 938 yards and seven touchdowns.

Names and numbers are important, but as usual there were intangibles that helped fuel their championship quest. While they may not have been obvious to start the season, they would emerge as a driving force and combined with its talent, lead Michigan to a national championship.

The Wolverines' defense served notice in the '97 opener against Colorado with four interceptions, one by Charles Woodson. The emerging star also caught a 29-yard pass in the 27-3 romp. In week two, Woodson was on the receiving end of a ten-yard touchdown from Griese. The game against Baylor showcased an explosive offense, which picked up 532 yards, leading to a dominating 38-3 victory.

By now it was becoming apparent that this team might be something special. It had risen to number six in the rankings, which wasn't hurt by a 21-14 win over Notre Dame. Indiana would be shutout 37-0 the following week. Northwestern was held to just two field goals, as Michigan's defense continued its domination of opponents, in a 23-6 victory for the Wolverines.

Iowa came into the Big House thinking upset and almost pulled it off after leading 21-7 at halftime. But Michigan countered with a couple of third quarter touchdowns to tie it, only to have the Hawkeyes regain the advantage in the fourth. Tim Dwight, who had already scored on a 61-yard punt return in the second quarter, took the kickoff back 72 yards and set up a 38 yard field goal by Zach Bromert, 24-21 Iowa. Brian Griese connected with Jerame Tuman with 2:55 left in the game, for a 28-24 Michigan advantage. It wasn't over until Sam Sword's interception with a half minute remaining. The Wolverines and their faithful could finally breathe a sigh of relief.

Next up the Spartans, who were averaging 34 points a contest. But six interceptions (a record for U of M), including two by Woodson and two more by Marcus Ray, proved to be too much for Michigan State to overcome. Michigan is a 23-7 winner, thanks in part to Kraig Baker's three field goals.

Minnesota was defeated 24-3, setting up a showdown with second ranked Penn State in Happy Valley. Michigan's defense set the tone early by sacking quarterback Mike McQueary twice on Penn State's first possession. On offense Griese hit Woodson for a 37-yard score, then found Tuman for another...sending the game into halftime with Michigan leading 24-0. Michigan's offense produced 416 yards in the game, while its defense held Penn State to zero third down conversions, sacked the quarterback five times, and had nine tackles for loss. 34-8 Wolverines, in dominant fashion, as Joe Paterno suffers his worst loss at home.

Wisconsin, playing at home, offered another tough challenge, but Michigan scored on its opening drive when Chris Howard went in from the one. The Wolverines never trailed. The touchdown was set up by a play that featured Griese throwing to Woodson, who threw back to Griese, who picked up 28 yards to the Badgers one-yard line. Woodson recorded his sixth interception, tops in the country. He also had three receptions for 28 yards, as Michigan rolled 26-16.

Every week another huge challenge, from a schedule considered the toughest among Division 1-A schools, based on records from the previous year. One game remained...the annual showdown with Ohio State. The Big House was loud, as fans agonized on practically every play. So much at stake...an undefeated season, the first since 1948, and a potential national championship hung in the balance.

Again, Charles Woodson showed why he was being considered the best in college football. He had a 37-yard reception from Griese, on Michigan's first scoring drive, a one yard run by Anthony Thomas. Then Woodson added a 78- yard punt return for a touchdown. It gave Michigan a 13-nothing advantage at the half. In the third quarter Woodson picked off his seventh pass of the season, stopping Ohio

State deep in Michigan territory. Andre Weathers added a 43-yard interception return for a touchdown, and Michigan had a 20-0 lead. The second ranked Wolverines held on to win 20-14...and were crowned Big Ten Champions!

The Winner! a Simple Declaration... but in Reality, is it?

Name the game and you could have almost as many winners as competitors. It just depends on the sport. But our subject is college football. Because the season can't be replayed, it will be forever debated; was Michigan or Nebraska the true national champ? In the Heisman Trophy voting, should it have been Charles Woodson or Peyton Manning?

The ballots for the Heisman were tallied before the bowl games and Woodson, much to the dismay of Tennessee fans, beat favorite son Manning, handing Woodson college football's top honor. Frankly, had the voting took place after the post season, I think it would have favored Woodson even more, considering the way Michigan and Tennessee finished.

I am a proud former defensive back, and applaud the voters, who finally gave those who play the positions, and on defense, their due. Yes, Woodson benefited from competing on offense, plus he was an extraordinary kick returner as well. When all that is considered, the ways he could impact a game, why not Woodson? An overwhelming majority of the voters felt the same way.

Actually, the outcome gave more credence to what the Heisman is supposed to reflect...the most outstanding player in college football. In 1997, according to writers across the county, except the South region, that was Charles Woodson. He is the first predominantly defensive player to capture the honor, and to that I say...about time.

As for the debate over who was the real national champion, Michigan or Nebraska? That conversation is just as tricky. The Wolverines over took Nebraska, November 10th (week 12) and moved into the number one ranking in the Associated Press Poll, following their convincing 34-8 victory over third- ranked and undefeated Penn State at Beaver Stadium. Prior to that game, the Nittany Lions owned the longest winning streak at 12 games.

However, the Coaches Poll favored Florida State, who replaced Nebraska as the top team that same week. Michigan was ranked second, Nebraska third. The Cornhuskers were also third in the A.P. Poll.

Two weeks later, Florida State dropped in the rankings after a 32-29 loss to arch-rival Florida. That elevated Nebraska to number two in the A.P. Poll behind Michigan, where it ended the year. In the Coaches Poll, Michigan took over the number one spot and Nebraska moved up to number two. The Wolverines had 53 ½ first place votes, to the Cornhuskers 8 ½, heading into the bowl games.

Michigan would beat seventh ranked Pac 10 champ Washington State 21-16, in the Rose Bowl. It was a highly competitive game which originally featured Michigan's defense against Washington State's Ryan Leaf and his five receiver offense. But it turned into an offensive show for both teams.

Leaf set records during the year with over 3,600 yards passing and 33 touchdowns. He was as good as advertised, throwing for 331 yards, fifth highest total in Rose Bowl history…and one touchdown. But Michigan quarterback Brian Griese, who was named the game's Most Valuable Player, threw for three touchdowns. Two ended up in the hands of Tai Streets, who caught four of Griese's passes for 127 yards.

In the Orange Bowl, Nebraska ran over Peyton Manning and third ranked (both polls) Tennessee 42-17. Manning was held to just 131 yards passing, while Nebraska picked up over 534 yards of offense, 409 on the ground. Ahman Green set a record by rushing for 201 yards and two touchdowns, and was named MVP of the game.

Three days later, it was revealed that while Michigan finished number one in the final Associated Press Poll, it had been over taken by Nebraska in the Coaches Poll…32 first place votes to 30. Since this was

Tom Osborne's last game as coach of the Cornhuskers, the prevailing thought among Michigan faithful was this was a sympathy vote for Osborne and his Cornhuskers.

This is a tough one for me to call, with both sides presenting legitimate arguments. In the end, it apparently came down to the dominant performance by Nebraska against Manning and Tennessee. It's hard to argue with that. For the record... no top ranked team, since the permanent post bowl game poll was established in 1968, has lost its position after winning in the post season in the A.P. Poll. Not so in the Coaches Poll. Georgia Tech ousted Colorado, thanks to a one point win over Notre Dame in the 1991 Orange Bowl. This led to our present day, College Football Playoff National Championship, which has its own set of problems trying to decide who is really number one. In 1997 Michigan did everything to state its case, that can't be argued.

In addition to Charles Woodson...Zach Adami, Brian Griese, Steve Hutchinson, Jon Jansen, Jerame Tuman, Marcus Ray, Glen Steele, Sam Sword, and Andre Waters would be either named All-Big Ten or All America, before leaving Ann Arbor. Running back Anthony Thomas was named the Big Ten Freshman of the year in 1997. Head Coach Lloyd Carr won, among others, the Walter Camp Coach of the Year Award. 31 Michigan players on the 1997 squad would compete in the National Football League.

From a players' perspective, even if you were competing in Pop Warner football, you will always remember an undefeated, unblemished season....especially if you weren't expected to accomplish it. I couldn't help but drift back to the fall of 1967 at Booker T. Washington, and our march to the Oklahoma State High School AAA Championship. It was a much smaller stage than the one Michigan starred on, but the similarities for me were evident 30 years later: success and satisfaction, realizing against all odds, you emerge number one!

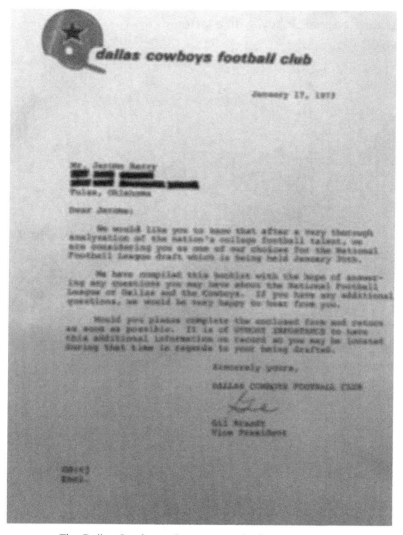

The Dallas Cowboys show interest before 1973 draft.

*St. Louis Cardinals follow with a letter.

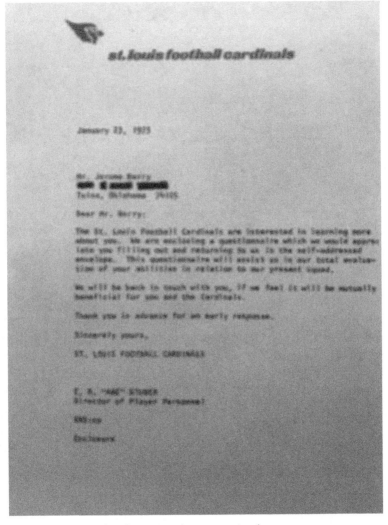

The dream just keeps getting better.

I tackle a new game.

Hello Houston!

Ray Miller my mentor. Tough but fair.

Robert (Bob) Brandon

Simply the best!

Jacques Cousteau. Legendary explorer of the oceans.

*Houston Oilers Receiver Kenny Burrough shows me his leaping ability.

Jay Berry's Sports Odyssey And Beyond

Jay Berry's odyssey: 'Black 14' to Ch. 7

sports on the air
Joe Lapointe

Political passion filled the air in the autumn of 1969. The Chicago Seven were on trial for disrupting the previous year's Democratic National Convention. Universities such as Wayne State in Detroit emptied while students marched in the streets against the Vietnam war. The assassination of Martin Luther King the year before had brought fresh anger and purpose to the American civil rights movement. Even sports, the toy department of life, became an ideological battlefield.

One skirmish occurred that October in Laramie, Wyo., where 14 black members of the undefeated Wyoming football team wanted to wear black armbands in protest before and during a game with Brigham Young.

They wanted to protest the beliefs of the Church of Jesus Christ of Latter-Day Saints (Mormon), which operates BYU. They said the religion had racist policies (some of which have since been changed) that treated blacks as inferior. They took their case first to their coach, Lloyd Eaton, who kicked them off the team, in part because "we do not build winning teams by debate."

Asked recently if he would do it again, Eaton — now a scout for the Green Bay Packers — replied: "They were biting the hand that feeds them . . . It was a very easy decision to make, and I'd make it over again."

Most of the "Black 14," as they were called, have done all right. One, Willie Hysaw, is co-ordinator of sales promotion for the Pontiac Division of General Motors in Pontiac. Another, Tony McGee, plays for the Washington Redskins.

And then there is Jay Berry, a defensive back who was known at Wyoming as "Jerry Berry." Berry, 31 now, was recently hired at Channel 7 (WXYZ-TV) as a sportscaster, anchoring on weekends and reporting during the week.

HE CAME from a Chicago station and he's now the only black sportscaster on Detroit's three major network-affiliated stations. (Charlie Neal, formerly of Channel 2, has moved to New York). Berry recalled the other day that "I still have my black armband," and he still has his memories.

"Yes, I would do it again," said Berry,

Free Press Photo

Jay Berry: "I don't feel I did anything wrong . . . You get bad raps for being in the wrong place at the wrong time."

who was courted briefly by the Dallas Cowboys 10 years ago. "I don't feel I did anything wrong. I was shocked when he

See SPORTS ON THE AIR, Page 6D

My welcome to Detroit.

CHAPTER 10

Barry, The Hitman, and The Queen

My first ten years in Detroit, the Lions had only two winning seasons, which helped give birth to the saying…"Same Old Lions." However, it didn't stop 82,000 fans from filling the Pontiac Silverdome. Every Sunday they would show up, expecting a miracle, fully realizing the odds were stacked against them. In 1988, the team opened with a victory, but promptly followed it with six straight defeats on its way…to its second consecutive, four-win season. The team was frustrated, as were the fans…and this reporter. To best illustrate the situation, I went to my music archives again and added "lowlights" from the season. The song was "Just Once," performed by James Ingram.

> "I did my best. But I guess my best wasn't good enough, 'cause here we are, back where we were before.
> Seems nothin' ever changes, we're back to being strangers, wondering if we ought to stay or head on out the door.
> Just once…can't we figure out what we keep doin' wrong. Why we never last for very long. What are we doin' wrong?"

You get the picture, as did Head Coach Darryl Rogers (he got the boot before the season was over), and especially the players, many of whom were not happy with my "video production" and let me know it. Can't say that I blame them, but there are only so many human interest, feel good stories during times like those.

In 1989, with the third selection in the NFL Draft...came hope, in the form of a 5'9", 200 pound running back, and the likes of which the National Football League had ever seen. Barry Sanders' impact was immediate and within two years of his arrival, my song for the team had changed to..."It's a Love Thing" by the Whispers.

Head Coach Wayne Fontes was handing out hugs, as if he was running for a political office. It caught on with the players, as the team enjoyed a 12-win season, an NFC Central Division Championship, and its second playoff win since 1957. Suddenly the impossible had become possible anytime number 20 touched the ball. His moves defied description, and how do you tackle someone like that? He reduced All-Pro players, the best of the best, into unwilling stooges in his endless highlight reels. What made him even more incredible was his demeanor on and off the field...he was humble beyond belief.

But Barry wasn't even his father's choice as the best running back to play the game. William Sanders would tell anyone it was Jim Brown! William Sanders' favorite college football team? Oklahoma. Barry of course went to Oklahoma State. William loved to talk. Barry? Only if he had to...even then his words were kept to a minimum. Their contrasting styles are brought up to try and understand how Barry evolved into the person he became.

Actually, it appeared to me that Shirley Ann, his mom, right down to her build...and inner religious strength, best reflected how and why Barry did what he did. He handed the ball to officials instead of jumping up and down or dancing and gyrating, before spiking the football. She, I believe, was the reason when I would ask Barry..."How did you make that cut? That stutter step, followed by the 360 degree spin and burst of speed...where did you get that from?" His reply, following a smile that spreads across his face, would be something like..."Oh, you like that? Good." Are you kidding me? That's it, after what I just saw? His joy, was leaving me and thousands of others with utter amazement, after having witnessed something for the first, and probably last time in our lives.

He was like money in the bank…at least 1500 yards rushing each season and ten touchdowns, while producing more gaping mouths, and frustrated defenders than you can count. In 1997, Barry outdid himself by gaining 2,053 yards on the ground, at the time only the third runner to reach the 2,000 yard mark. He had help for sure, but his teammates, and the rest of the world, will admit Sanders deserved a lion's share (pun intended) of the credit. Because of him and Michigan's championship march, I was on what seemed like a daily shuttle between Ann Arbor and Pontiac for reaction.

Barry's exploits and consistency (he was rarely injured), allowed us to believe he would continue to play indefinitely. Granted, running backs take a pounding and careers are cut short because of the punishment. But Barry? Defenders never seemed to get a clean shot at him and he was in his prime, just 31 years old. Then, seemingly out of the blue, he was gone, leaving fans looking confused and feeling like some of his would be tacklers. He put in his ten…and that was the end.

In some ways we shouldn't have been surprised. Winning the rushing title as a rookie, which he could have done had he gone back into a game for another play or two, wasn't important to him. Neither was breaking Walter Payton's all-time NFL record for yards gained on the ground. The future Hall of Famer was dismayed at the direction the team was headed after the Lions started unloading quality players, many of them his friends. Often he was encouraged by his teammates to talk to the front office about his feelings, knowing Barry's voice carried a lot of weight. But apparently he never did.

He became frustrated and a "communications gap" opened. Barry was quoted as saying, "It was tough to stay focused and motivated." After all he had done, and the appearance that management no longer cared about winning "slammed me harder than any linebacker had ever hit me in my entire career," said Barry.

While I hated to see him go, an exit he later admitted could have been executed better, I was happy that he didn't leave broke. Anybody who knew anything about him, knew that was a distinct impossibility.

Sanders' frugal nature was legendary. Instead of having to return a $7.3 million dollar lump sum signing bonus to the Lions…an arbitrator ruled that only $1.8 million was required from Barry each year he didn't report to camp. Presumably, over the remaining four years of his contract, a good stock market could sweeten the ruling even more for number 20.

Reflecting, I've come to realize how fortunate I was to have had the opportunity to report on four of the best running backs ever to play in the National Football League. Earl Campbell, Walter Payton, Billy Sims, and Barry Sanders were not only in the record books, each was unique off the gridiron as well. Their compelling charisma, in addition to their humble nature, made them special people to encounter. They were approachable super stars, who delivered what both young and old fans expected out of their heroes…a welcoming smile, time for a quick picture or autograph, words of encouragement, and affirmation that the next big game would be a win for the home team!

THE HITMAN

Boxing can be barbaric, bloody, and yet beautiful all in the same three-minute round. Through the centuries, some fans of the fisticuffs even took to calling it the "sweet science." It can be debated as to how and when that started, but the great "Sugar" Ray Robinson's success made him the poster-boy for the phrase, during his many championship bouts. He dissected his opponents' fighting style and adapted… one round brawling, counter punching the next, and possibly followed with an exhibition of his jab.

Cassius Clay took the sport to a whole new level in 1960, when he returned from the Rome Summer Olympics with the heavyweight gold medal. His upset of Heavyweight Champ, Sonny Liston in 1964, gave him his first professional title and a platform to announce his conversion to the Nation of Islam. In the process, he changed his name to Muhammad Ali. He also changed boxing too by making fights look easy at times…and opponents foolish. Ali talked a good game, "Float like a butterfly, sting like a bee. Rumble young man rumble!" And he backed it up, while dodging missiles to his mug.

Boxing has lost most of its luster, as competing sports like Mixed Martial Arts (MMA), the retirement and deaths of fighters, trainers, and managers…have taken their toll. But when I arrived in Detroit, it was a much different story. The importance and popularity of the sport here is as obvious as that 8,000 pound dark bronzed fist that sits in the middle of Downtown. Sports Illustrated magazine commissioned it to be sculpted, and presented it as a monument to the city and favorite son, Joe Louis, in 1986. He was the World Heavyweight Champ from 1937 to 1949.

In 1980, Thomas Hearns, "The Hitman," manager-trainer Emanuel Steward, and the Kronk gym were known worldwide. Hearns was a devastating puncher, and was voted fighter of the year after taking the World Boxing Association welterweight crown from Pipino Cuevas. The following year, Hearns fought and lost to "Sugar" Ray Leonard, the World Boxing Council Welterweight Champ, in a 1981 classic. Leonard would later retire because of a detached retina in his right eye. There would be no rematch until 1989.

Hearns moved up in weight and captured the WBC Super Welterweight title from Wilfred Benitez in 1982, thanks to a 15-round majority decision. Two years later, he scored a second round technical knockout against Roberto Duran at Caesars Palace.

In 1985, Hearns stepped up in weight again and challenged undisputed Middleweight Champ, "Marvelous" Marvin Hagler. The fight, especially the first round, is considered one of the greatest in the history of the sport. It was rightly titled, "The War." Hearns was hoping to use his height and reach advantage, but from the opening bell, Hagler turned it into a brawl, much to the dismay of Hearns' trainer Emanuel Steward. Later it was learned that Hearns broke his right hand during one of the violent exchanges. Hagler suffered a cut on his forehead, but the heavy blows continued, as the two fighters threw caution to the wind.

Hearns would later admit in addition to breaking his right hand, "That first round took everything I had, man." The second round revealed as much. Hearns stumbled several times while trying to turn the match into one that featured more movement and boxing. But Tommy's legs were clearly gone and Hagler's switch from orthodox style, then back to his normal southpaw stance, helped to inflict further damage on Hearns.

It appeared that the tables were turning in round three, when referee Richard Steele stopped the action a minute into the round. Hagler's cut on his forehead had opened up and blood was flowing heavily. The fight was allowed to go on, but realizing that it could be stopped at any time, Hagler returned to an aggressive style and attacked Hearns, sending him to the canvas after a vicious right to the chin. Britain's Boxing News magazine called the fight "Eight Minutes of Mayhem" and it won the fight of the year award, although it lasted only three rounds.

Hagler had worked his plan to perfection, realizing Hearns' reach, height, and boxing capability didn't favor him. Hagler also knew "The Hitman" didn't get his nickname by accident and Tommy's intimidating style could help lure him into the kind of battle that Hagler thought he could win. He was right.

These welterweight and middleweight fights of the 80's are legendary. They helped steal much of the thunder away from the heavyweights, especially since Ali was on the brink of retirement. Thomas "Hitman" Hearns, "Sugar" Ray Leonard, "Marvelous" Marvin Hagler, Roberto "Hands of Stone" Duran, John "The Beast" Mugabi, and Iran Barkley among others, kept fight fans salivating for the next showdown. When Leonard announced he was returning to the ring in 1983, it only made things sweeter.

Leonard got past Kevin Howard, via a ninth round technical knockout in 1984. The fight was postponed three months, when the ex-champ had corrective surgery on his damaged right eye. During the bout, Leonard suffered the first knockdown of his professional career and shocked everyone by announcing he would retire again. This one lasted almost three years, until the money and the challenge became too much to ignore.

The match against Marvin Hagler was promoted as the "Super Fight." It guaranteed $11 million for Leonard and $12 million for a heavily favored Hagler. It took place April 6, 1987, at Caesars Palace. Leonard was one of the announcers for the Hearns-Hagler fight and realized Tommy's mistake of trying to brawl with Hagler. That oddly had been Leonard's initial plan, but he wisely thought differently the night of the fight.

Unlike the way he looked against Hearns, Hagler appeared tentative and stiff, compared to the speedy Leonard, who took the early rounds. But Hagler started to dominate in the fifth and sixth. In the end however, Leonard scored a twelfth- round, controversial split-decision win. It kept intact his undefeated streak in Las Vegas. In fact, his 1980 loss to Roberto Duran in Montreal was the only blemish on his record, which he redeemed in Duran's infamous "No Mas" fiasco, five months later in New Orleans.

Hearns, "The Motor City Cobra" (his preferred nickname), kept busy piling up wins over James Shuler and Mark Medal, retaining the WBC middleweight title in the process. He beat Doug Dewitt, then won the WBC Light Heavyweight Championship, thanks to a tenth-round technical knockout of Dennis Andries. Hearns added the vacant WBC middleweight crown by knocking out Juan Roldan in the fourth round October 29, 1987.

Seven months later, Hearns suffered "The upset of the year," when Iran Barkley pulled off a third-round technical knockout against Hearns, who lost his WBC middleweight title. Before 1988 ended however, Hearns' twelve round decision over James "The Heat" Kinchen gave him the World Boxing Organization Super Middleweight Championship, setting the stage for his long awaited rematch against "Sugar" Ray Leonard.

It would take place June 12th, 1989, at Caesars Palace. For eight long years Hearns had endured questions about the first fight: how

Leonard had not only beaten him, but in many ways caused him to question himself. In his mind it was time for redemption...an opportunity to silence the demons and inquiring minds, once and for all. He would fight smarter and show the naysayers he was the better fighter. Hearns was guaranteed $11 million, Leonard $14 million.

There is nothing like a fight crowd and the one that converged on Las Vegas for "Hearns - Leonard Two" had to be seen, to be believed. The celebrities, rappers, millionaires, and wannabes, their clothes, outrageous jewelry, expensive cars, and extensive entourages, were like nothing I had experienced. It was crazy in and around Vegas...but especially at Caesars. It was a who's who parade, that didn't stop at some imaginary "red carpet." It continued to the shops, where "must have" items were waiting to be snatched up, the price was no problem. On to the restaurants...where fans were feasting as if they were at the legendary emperor's table, and eventually to the pool, the ultimate place to see...and be seen.

Hearns and trainer Emanuel Steward did themselves and the city of Detroit proud, in the way they reached out to the fight fans. Some of them were youngsters, who were invited into the ring to "spar" with Thomas, and exercise with the champ. It was a public relations dream display, by showing Hearns in a much different light than the "all business and serious" fighter they saw during an actual bout.

The scene was calculated and necessary, because Leonard became a media darling when he returned from the 1976 Montreal Olympics with a gold medal in the light welterweight division. However, Leonard's circumstances were not as sweet as they may have appeared outwardly. He was facing a paternity suit, and potential endorsement deals evaporated when that became public, plus both his parents were suddenly unable to work because of medical issues.

In the ring Leonard displayed, as he did in his first fight with Hearns, that he had heart, and a flair for the dramatic...often putting together a flurry of punches at the exact moment necessary to sway the judges and the crowd. He was very good at this, a savvy showman. No one knew that better than Hearns, who also knew Leonard's popularity was strongest in Las Vegas, where he had never lost.

Over in Los Angeles, the Pistons were in the process of sweeping the Lakers out of the NBA Finals, and winning their first championship. How unbelievable it would be if one of Motown's favorite sons captures a boxing crown the day before? That thought, was almost too much for me to comprehend. I had been in Las Vegas for a week, doing "live" reports back to Detroit on the workouts and detailing, practically every movement of the boxers.

The actual day of the fight was the most critical of all. A lot of what I had done previously, exclusive interviews and workout footage, required me to "toss" or do an "on camera" lead to an insert, that I would send back to channel 7 . This would allow me to show presence from the location, because interviews at this point had been stopped until after the fight. A major problem developed that could sabotage everything! The Las Vegas sun had "fried" some of the internal components of the camera.

It is a very unique piece of equipment, and even with all the networks and stations covering the fight, I couldn't find a replacement! You can't just go to the local RadioShack and have it repaired or have another sent from who knows where? L.A. would be the closest possibility, but there wasn't enough time to locate one and have it shipped before our evening broadcasts. I was in a huge panic and in need of a miracle. Thankfully, at the last minute, I found one in a network technician, who was able to dissect and repair the camera, and I just happened to have an extra $300 on me…to make it worth his time. Whew!

It was an idyllic night for a fight. The heat of the day had given way to a cool delightful June evening. The capacity crowd of 15,300 fans gathered in the make-shift outdoor stadium, and a worldwide closed circuit audience would soon get the show they had long anticipated. But no one looked forward to this night more than Hearns. However, there would be more on his mind than just his long- awaited rematch with Leonard.

Earlier, Hearns learned that his younger brother, Henry, was charged with first degree murder. Henry was accused of shooting his 19-year old fiancé. She had been found, shot once in the head, by a gun belonging to Thomas, in a bedroom of a home owned by Thomas. Henry was convicted of second-degree murder November 22, 1989, and sentenced to 25 to 50 years in prison. Three years later, it was reported Thomas agreed to pay the woman's family $650,000 to settle a wrongful death lawsuit. Henry was released from prison February 20, 2015.

Tommy had a lot to think about, but he wasn't about to lose sight of Leonard, and as Hearns was quoted as saying..."Eight years of pain, with a little monster following me around." Gone was his Jheri curl, which in the Hagler fight accentuated every blow when Marvin connected. Hearns was taking every precaution, and not nearly as many chances, as in previous fights.

Leonard, the WBC Super Welterweight Champ at 160, was 2 ½ pounds lighter than Hearns, and a 3-1 favorite to beat Tommy, the WBC No.1 ranked super middleweight contender. Hearns was also the World Boxing Organization Super Middleweight Champion, but that title was not at stake.

Hearns took control early. In the third round, he staggered Leonard with a right hand...followed by another, sending Leonard to the canvas floor, although some critics saw it more of a nudge than a punch. Leonard survived and inflicted damage of his own in the fourth and fifth, stunning Hearns and thrilling the crowd. Back and forth they would go, Hearns on the assault early in the seventh, only to have Leonard return like that little monster Tommy referred to earlier. But this was real. No one had to convince either fighter of that. In the eleventh, Hearns would drop Leonard again, then hang on in the dramatic twelfth, when once again Leonard finished with a flurry.

I got up from my seat and held my breath, realizing in my mind, with no "homer" inclination...that Tommy had clearly won the fight, and exacted a large degree of redemption. But how would the judges see it? I was stunned and shocked when it was ruled a draw, as thousands in the stands screamed their disapproval...to put it politely! Tommy, in the post-fight news conference, seemed relieved that he hadn't lost. But by the next day, after having a chance to review the fight, Hearns came to the same conclusion as the irate spectators, he had clearly won. Some years later, even Leonard admitted Hearns deserved the win.

Thomas Hearns was the first boxer to win world titles in four weight divisions and was inducted into the International Boxing Hall of Fame in 2012.

Go Green...Go White!

During the late 1990's and the early 2000's...Flint, (about an hour Northwest of Detroit) was known, not for its water crisis...but for the talented basketball players that landed on Michigan State's roster. Antonio Smith, Mateen Cleaves, Charlie Bell, and Morris Peterson became known as "The Flintstones" because of their home town and success on the court. They would guide the Spartans to three consecutive NCAA Final Four appearances. To fully appreciate that bit of trivia, consider that only Duke and UCLA have surpassed that streak.

Head Coach Tom Izzo had not only assembled some impressive players, but a coaching staff as well. Tom Crean, Stan Heath, Mike Garland, and Brian Gregory would all become head coaches and form a loyal, tight-knit group cultivated by their enthusiastic, and at times ballistic leader. Izzo preached tough defense and rebounding by getting into the players faces and their psyche. It all payed off during the 1999-2000 season.

Unlike the previous year, when they won both the Big Ten regular season championship outright, and the conference tournament, this time the Spartans shared the league title with Ohio State, but again reigned as tournament champs. Iowa, Wisconsin, and Illinois fell in succession at Chicago's United Center and Michigan State entered the NCAA Tournament as the No.1 seed in the Midwest region.

Impressive credentials for sure, but it was also a "been there, done that" scenario that ended with the Spartans falling short against Duke in the 1999 title game. That feeling of coming up short was hard to kick for Izzo, and his players. But it also served as huge motivation for this season. Extended early morning workouts in the summer? Check. Solidifying players' roles? Check. Pushing past the daily physical scrimmages? Check. Forming an unbreakable bond as a team? Check. Everything that needed to be done to insure there would be a change in this year's script, was addressed...and it showed.

Top seeded MSU started its quest in Cleveland against the Crusaders of Valparaiso. A tall team, but not very talented. Valparaiso fell behind 29-15 at the half and would finish with only 38 points, to 65 for Michigan State. Mateen Cleaves scored 15 points and had eight assists.

Utah, the second opponent, would offer more of a challenge. In fact, the Utes enjoyed a three point advantage at halftime. Both teams would hit over half of their shots, but the Spartans' second half explosion was too much for Utah, who would lose 73-61. Cleaves' 21 points and Andre Hutson's 19 enabled MSU to keep its Sweet Sixteen date at The Palace of Auburn Hills, where expectant fans were waiting to greet their favorite team.

Syracuse was also waiting. The Orangemen, seeded fourth, seized control early and enjoyed a double digit lead, before Michigan State went on an unbelievable 15-0 run. The Spartans outscored Syracuse 51-24 in the second half and knocked the Orangemen out of the tourney, 75 to 58. Here's a stat for you: Michigan States' starters accounted for all but two of the team's points. All five scored in double figures and Morris Peterson "Mo Pete" threw in five triples and 21 points.

The Elite Eight contest with Iowa State was expected to be a tough one...and it was. The Cyclones were also a team on a mission, just like all the tournament competitors. Iowa State enjoyed a seven-point cushion with 5:30 left in the contest. However the Spartans, urged on by their green-clad fans, closed with a 23-5 spurt to advance 75-64, and reach their second consecutive Final Four. A.J Granger and Mo Pete led all scorers with 18 apiece.

Wisconsin had already surprised a No.1 seed, and would love nothing better than upsetting conference foe MSU, thus preventing the Spartans from reaching the finals and a possible championship. Nothing personal? Consider this, Wisconsin lost twice to Michigan State during the regular season, then was knocked out of the semi-finals of the Big Ten Tournament by MSU. So you might say there was desire for a little payback stuck in the Badgers' craw...just a little!

The defensive match-up was expected to be similar to being parked at a red light...that is stuck: like spending a lifetime, one afternoon, at the Secretary of State's (DMV) office, like being put on endless hold while trying to reach a "live" technician, as that "music" drones on. Might as well drive to Alaska...at least you would be getting somewhere.

So those visualizing this sadistic scenario weren't surprised when the scoreboard revealed only 36 points had been scored by halftime... that's a combined total for both teams! Michigan State shot just 25% from the floor, Wisconsin 29%.

Thankfully, they picked up the pace in the second half, which favored the Spartans. MSU would finally have its much sought-after return to the championship game, after a hard fought 53-41 victory. Over 43,000 glass-eyed fans were witnesses in Indianapolis' RCA Dome. Mo Pete's 20 points topped MSU, who now had only Florida standing in its way from the school's second national championship!

Michigan State would never trail in the contest, but it wasn't without drama, especially when Cleaves limped to the locker room with a serious ankle injury early in the second half. MSU held a 50-44 advantage and Cleaves had tossed in 18. Although he did return, Cleaves wouldn't score again. But Mo Pete, who would lead the Spartans with 21, along with the rest of the team, picked up the slack, as Michigan State held off the determined Gators 89-76.

Success is sweet, saddened by a short shelf life. Should you be so fortunate, make the most of it, cherish it, and realize...paradise is not pretense. If you can't appreciate it, check your pulse! It's a little something that has occurred to me over the years. I believe every champion, and competitor would agree.

It is one of the more memorable moments during my career. Not only because of their NCAA Championship, but the sacrifices and teamwork it took for Michigan State to reach its goal. The Spartans' hard work and totally unselfish attitude should serve as a model for athletic teams and businesses as well. Individual accomplishments and achievements can't guarantee ultimate satisfaction, when more than one person is involved.

2004...Un-Likely Parts Drive Pistons

The Pistons know a little something about that, and in 2004 would serve as a good example of how a team can succeed, while individuals fall short. Joe Dumars, one of my favorites from the Bad Boys era, found value in other team's discards and blended the Pistons into a cohesive roster. The players realized how they were being perceived, which gave them motivation to prove others wrong. Dumars was betting on it, and more often than not he was right.

After he retired and became the Pistons' President of Basketball Operations, one of the first things Dumars did was trade former teammate Grant Hill to Orlando for Chucky Atkins and Ben Wallace. On paper it didn't make sense to anybody but Dumars, who realized Hill was planning on leaving. So why not get something for him, rather than just letting his all-star walk away? Atkins gave his all, but was no Grant Hill. However, Ben Wallace would become what the team stood for: hard work, tough defense, and a blue collar attitude.

Two years later, Dumars would send Jerry Stackhouse to Washington in exchange for Richard "Rip" Hamilton. He would sign Chauncey Billups, who had bounced around from Boston, to Toronto, to Denver, then Minnesota. That same year, 2002, Dumars drafted lanky Tayshaun Prince out of the University of Kentucky. Rick Carlisle, NBA Coach of The Year in 2002, would be let go after the 2003 season and replaced by the well-traveled Larry Brown.

This was proof Dumars was a man on a mission…or one crazy executive, with an addiction for making deals, because those mentioned were but a small number Dumars pulled off after becoming the Pistons leader, and he wasn't close to being finished.

He had returned the Pistons back to the post season, but after being swept by New Jersey in the 2003 Eastern Conference Finals, Dumars realized he was still missing an important piece to his puzzle. Midway of the 2004 season he got him, in the person of 6'11" Rasheed Wallace. It was another gamble by Dumars, probably the biggest one yet, because Rasheed came with a trunk full of baggage, well documented during his career. He picked up technical fouls the way Motown collected hits. But he could also be a nightmare for opponents.

With Chauncey Billups distributing to teammates, "Rip" Hamilton scoring off screens…like a machine, Rasheed Wallace dunking down low, Tayshaun Prince using his 7'2" wingspan to harass opponents, and "Big Ben" Wallace, a future Defensive Player of the Year controlling the boards…the Pistons were dangerous. Add a bench that included a young Mehmet Okur, Corliss Williamson, Lindsey Hunter, Elden Campbell, and Mike James, they become legitimate contenders, led by a Hall of Fame coach.

Still, the Pistons would finish seven games behind the Indiana Pacers in the Eastern Conference Central Division, and end up the third seed, heading into the playoffs. The Milwaukee Bucks presented the first challenge, and it didn't appear to be much of one after a 26-point blowout in game one. But Milwaukee took game two, 92-88 and in the process, stole home court advantage. Consider it a wakeup call for Detroit and its defensive-minded players, who put the clamps on the Bucks by winning the next three games in double digit fashion.

The New Jersey Nets, who swept the Pistons in last season's Eastern Conference Finals, quickly realized this was a different scenario when they were routed 78-56 in game one of their Eastern Conference Semifinal series. It was the second-lowest point total in NBA playoff history. Game two featured more of the same as Detroit rolled to a 95-80 victory.

But the Nets reversed their fortunes after leaving The Palace. The offense of Richard Jefferson…then Jason Kidd, enabled New Jersey to storm back and tie the series, setting up a memorable three overtime thriller in game five. Again, Jefferson was the main man for the Nets, scoring 18 points after regulation, but the team's unlikely hero was Brian Scalabrine. He threw in a career-high 17 points, after having scored a total of 19 previously in the playoffs. New Jersey's 127-120 victory at The Palace had the Nets poised to close the series out in East Rutherford.

Having come back from a two-game deficit, and now leading three games to two, had the Nets and their fans feeling pretty confident that at least one more win was a distinct possibility. A lot of the East Coast media fueled those thoughts, but the Pistons remained loose and confident. Rip Hamilton's 24 points, scoring from a reliable bench, and the Pistons defense led to an 81-75 victory and a return to The Palace for a dramatic game seven.

Just like game one, the Pistons defense was too much for New Jersey, which was held to just 69 points. Offensively, (Mr. Big Shot) Chauncey Billups and Rip Hamilton had 22 and 21 points respectively…and Ben Wallace's 18 points were a welcomed surprise. As for New Jersey, Jason Kidd was scoreless in the post season for the first time in his career. The Pistons advance to their second straight trip to the Eastern Conference Finals 90-69. Next up, Reggie Miller, former Head Coach Rick Carlisle, and the Indiana Pacers.

In Carlisle's first season, the Pacers captured the Central Division title and set a franchise record with 61 wins…which gave them home court advantage. Boosted by that and a tiebreaking three pointer by Miller (his only basket) with 31 seconds left, Indiana took game one…78-74.

But in his typical fashion, Rasheed Wallace dropped a hint regarding the outcome in game two..."They will not win game two. You can quote me on the front page, on the back page, anywhere you want. They will not win game two."

It is one thing "to talk it," backing it up can be daunting...or just not possible. But 'Sheed and his defensive-minded partners put on a display by swatting away 19 shots by the Pacers, the second highest total in NBA playoff history. The biggest block, delivered by Tayshaun Prince, sealed a 72-67 victory for the Pistons and left Reggie Miller talking to himself. There would be no last second heroics as in game one. Miller had what he thought was a game-tying breakaway basket late in the contest, only to have Prince seemingly come out of nowhere to knock the ball away. It was the fourth block in the game for Prince. The Wallaces...Rasheed and Ben, combined for 13. The Pistons had ended Indiana's 14-game home winning streak and headed to Auburn Hills with home court advantage, and the series tied at one.

Game three featured Rasheed's offense. He tied Rip Hamilton with 20 points as the Pistons grabbed an 85-78 victory and a 2-1 series advantage. The Pacers made a series of it again by holding the Pistons to just 68 points in game four. But there would be no joy in their return to Indy, as Rip got loose for 33 points in game five. 83-65 Pistons, who look to close it out at The Palace.

It was another defensive struggle with neither team scoring 70 points. Some might call it an ugly victory, but you can also call the Pistons...Eastern Conference Champions. The 69-65 win sends them into the NBA Finals for the first time in 14 years. The Los Angeles Lakers would be waiting.

A Fitting Exit...for me and the Pistons

Like a script from an aging athlete's story...I didn't see it coming, but the 2004 NBA Finals would bring an end to my 31 years in broadcasting. Channel 7 and I would part company. Truth be told, it didn't come as a total shock. For a few years, the last couple of contract negotiations indicated my future at WXYZ could be in doubt. You generally don't get a job in this business unless someone else leaves. I realized that very early in my career with each move I made. In retrospect, I couldn't think of a better way to exit...covering a world championship! Since I didn't know it would be my finale, I could just enjoy it and its improbable outcome...sort of like my career.

The setting at the Staples Center, scene for the opening two games of the series, brought the stars out with their glitz, glamour and Cartier sunglasses. It was the place to be seen and celebrate the heavily-favored Lakers' fourth title in five years. The team featured Kobe Bryant, one of the most exciting players in the NBA, and clogging up the middle, a mountain of a man in 7'1"...326 pound Shaquille O'Neal, the most dominant big man in the game. In addition, to assist in this season's championship quest, Los Angeles added All-Stars Karl Malone and Gary Payton. With this group and a capable bench, Head Coach Phil Jackson seemed assured of his tenth ring.

On paper, assurances can disappear like the ink that prints them... as the Lakers would soon learn. The Pistons ambushed them in game one with the same trademark defense that suffocated previous opponents. Los Angeles put up 73 shots, but found the mark on only 29... just 39% shooting as a team. Kobe Bryant was 10 of 27 from the floor, to score 25 points. Shaq however was basically unstoppable, missing only three shots and led both teams with 34 points. No other Laker scored in double figures. The Pistons' balanced scoring was topped by Chauncey Billups with 22. Detroit stole game one, 87-75 and served notice to both the Lakers and their fans...your celebration will have to be delayed, if it happens at all.

The Pistons had the Lakers' attention, now what? I'm thinking, seated comfortably at press row, keep on...keeping on! No team had bounced back to win a title after losing the first two games at home, so the pressure was squarely on Los Angeles and Kobe Bryant in particular. Yet, with time running out in game two, the Pistons were moments away from another improbable victory.

Just over two seconds remained with the Pistons clinging to a three point lead, when Kobe launched a desperation three pointer. Like so many times before, he buried the basket, forcing overtime and sending the crowd into a wild celebration. The Lakers would escape by dominating the extra period, limiting the Pistons to just two points in a 99-91 victory.

The Pistons and their fans were devastated. The prevailing feeling was that Los Angeles would now seize control of the series and eventually win. I saw things differently and said as much during our broadcast following the game, which included former Pistons Coach Chuck Daly back in our Southfield studios. I felt the Lakers were extremely fortunate and the Pistons could finish them off during the three games at The Palace. It was obvious to me that the only player the Pistons had real trouble stopping was Shaq, and as he said to anyone who would listen, he couldn't get the ball enough. Kobe wanted to be the main man and that left Shaq as a secondary option at best. It was a situation that would manifest itself for all to see by the time this series ended.

Back home, the Pistons became defensive-minded and shut down both Kobe and Shaq in game three. Once again they were the only Lakers to score in double figures, but could only manage a combined 25 points. Rip Hamilton's 31 easily surpassed their production and Chauncey Billups added 19, in an 88-68 romp by the Pistons. Total domination in this one as they controlled the action from start to finish. Thanks to the long arms and tenacity of Tayshaun Prince, Kobe was held scoreless in the first half and had just 11 points in the contest, and Shaq 14.

Game four featured the reemergence offensively of Rasheed Wallace. The fiery forward stayed out of foul trouble and led the Pistons with 26 points, and tied Ben Wallace with 13 rebounds. Shaq and Kobe bounced back with 36 and 20 points respectively. Shaq also pulled down 20 rebounds, but for the fourth consecutive game, they were the only Lakers with double figures. Suddenly the Pistons, a team some thought would have trouble winning one game…were one victory away from a title.

If L.A. was hoping for a letdown by Detroit in game five, it was sadly mistaken. Propelled by a raucous crowd, the Pistons never wavered. They were too much for the Lakers and proved what a team could accomplish. On this night, it was more obvious than ever, as all of Detroit's starters had 11 or more points, led by Rip Hamilton's 21. Chauncey Billups, wearing the uniform of his fifth team, was the MVP of the series.

The five games exposed just how heated the feud had grown between Shaq and Kobe. It spilled over into the front office. Phil Jackson was not retained as coach and Shaq, who asked to be traded, was sent to Miami.

CHAPTER 11

Life Through My Rear View Mirror... With the Head Beams Focused on God

"REVEREND PREACHER BERRY!" ONE OF my high school teammates gave me that title when I refused to accompany him and some others on a "shopping spree." They were going to rip off a store, and even if I wasn't going to participate, they wanted my shirt size hoping to return with something that would appeal to me. I wasn't the same person I was some years back, when a similar situation with my cousin had an owner of a store screaming..."Bring me back my pies!" I returned them, feeling embarrassed and ashamed, realizing I wasn't cut out for this. My religious upbringing taught me it wasn't something a Christian would do.

I was baptized at an early age, around eight or nine. I gave my life to Jesus Christ and it has changed me...forever. Unfortunately it didn't mean I would suddenly become perfect and live a sinless life, but God and his teachings gave me a moral compass, and I knew thievery should not be included in a Christian's DNA.

Through prayer and the Bible's teachings, I have come to know and believe in Christ...realizing all things are possible through Him. I accept He was the last sinless person, and no matter how hard I try to lead a totally righteous life, I will come up short of my goal. But I know what is expected of me and failure usually brings undesired consequences. On the other hand, I know God only wants the best for us and He continually proves that to me.

Someone once asked me, and I'm paraphrasing… "Why do we have to experience tough times, before we turn to God?" I didn't have an answer then and I thought about it for a while. In time I have come to realize God often has to get our attention before He can lift us up. Generally when things are going great for us, we make the mistake of thinking we are "large and in charge," that we are the reason for our good fortune…and nothing could be further from the truth. When we are facing life changing situations, possibly including a time-sensitive obstacle, we are forced to realize it is only through His grace that we have persevered…and sometimes even prospered.

Often as an athlete, I knew something I accomplished on the gridiron or basketball court seemingly came out of nowhere. The results and timing went far beyond my intentions (especially since I didn't know what I was about to do in the first place). The same can be said for my life in general…too many blessings for this man to think…I'm all that. I've also learned God has a sense of humor, believe it or not. When in need, right down to my last 53 cents…He has provided, and I can't help but smile and laugh…followed by a sincere, thank you Jesus!

RESPECTING THE QUEEN 1942-2018

They buried the queen yesterday, following an eight hour funeral attended by religious dignitaries, politicians, including former President Bill Clinton, musical greats, family, friends, and just common folk. It was befitting the Queen of Soul…filled with songs, laughter, more than a few tears, and memories that have spoken to all of us at one time or another…thanks to Aretha Franklin.

You could not ignore her, or her voice. Whether she was demanding "Respect" and in the process telling you to "Think," or just asking you to "Call Me," she did it in a way that stays with you…through the good times and the bad. In the process she collected 18 Grammys, received a star on the Hollywood Walk of Fame, was inducted into the Rock & Roll Hall of Fame, the NAACP Image Awards Hall of Fame, and the Apollo Theater Legends Walk of Fame. She performed at the inauguration of three presidents.

There were over 100 pink Cadillacs lining Seven Mile Road outside Greater Grace Church where the funeral was held. After being off the charts for a while, she hit it big again with "Freeway of Love" in 1985. The lyrics painted a picture of Aretha riding around in a pink Cadillac, but she wasn't alone.

> *"Knew you'd be a vision in white,*
> *How'd you get your pants so tight?*
> *Don't know what you're doin'*
> *But you must be livin' right, yeah!*

In the song's video, I was the driver of the pink Cadillac. I couldn't help but reflect back on, not only making the video, but having the privilege of being in it. Here's something I find funny…I never received any money for my appearance, but later realized countless men would have paid to sit next to Aretha in that video! Crazy huh? It became a huge hit, and although we didn't finish shooting until about three in the morning, few of my experiences can top that one.

Aretha, beyond her music, exemplified the Motown magic that is often shown in the people of Detroit. Granted, it can be a tough place like any major city, but there is a lot of love and forgiveness here too. When you're taken in by its people…Black, White, Chaldean, or Hispanic, you become one of them and they don't take kindly to others disparaging you.

Call it an "us against the world" kind of mentality, which I believe has evolved because of the years of negative comments, rightly or wrongly, heaped on Detroit. If you can't say something nice about the "D"…don't say it at all, and definitely don't say it around here.

I was introduced to Aretha by her niece, Sabrina, who I met at a social function. Her mother is Erma Franklin, who I already respected because of her own musical talents. Turns out Aretha was a channel 7 viewer. I was blown away by my good fortune and before I knew it, I was being invited to Aretha's legendary parties, which led to me driving that pink Cadillac in the video.

Watching her funeral, which was carried live locally, caused me to pause and reflect on what she meant to so many people. The whole week was dedicated to honoring her. Chene Park, a 5,000 seat waterfront amphitheater that faces the Detroit River and Windsor, Canada… has been renamed, "Aretha Franklin Park." Hearing testimonies about her: how she empowered people of all races…and women in particular, filled me up emotionally. I am thankful to have known her.

I can also say that about so many in Detroit and the surrounding area. The Pistons' Chuck Daly, Will Robinson, Owner Bill Davidson, the Lions' Wayne Fontes and Owner William Clay Ford, the Tigers' Sparky Anderson and Ernie Harwell, the Red Wings' Jacques Demers and Owner Mike Ilitch, who also owned the Detroit Tigers.

The college coaches, through wins and losses, also enhanced my life. People like Bo Schembechler, George Perles, Tom Izzo, Lloyd Carr, Perry Watson, Greg Kampe, Red Berenson, and Ron Mason. From the high school ranks, the late Ron Thompson and Elbert Richmond, Al Fracassa, John Harrington, Ben Kelso, Greg Carter, Brenda Gatlin, Jim Reynolds, Thomas Wilcher, and so many others, including the athletes.

And not to be forgotten, the incomparable Jackie Kallen. She's an extraordinary person who doesn't shy away from anything or anyone, including some of the most powerful men in – and out – of the boxing ring.

While sports was my main reason for coming to Detroit, a man needs a way to relax and the music in Motown offered plenty, even though Berry Gordy had relocated to Los Angeles. I was surprised to hear and see local talent like Norma Jean Bell, Kimmie Horne, and Thornetta Davis to name a few. On special nights, I might also be treated to some of the Motown greats who would drop in for a jam session. I can only imagine what it was like when so many of the great groups and individual stars were emerging here…like Jackie Wilson, Mary Wells, the Temptations, the Supremes, Smokey Robinson and the Miracles, the Four Tops, the Marvelettes, Martha and the Vandellas, the Spinners, and the Dramatics.

I had no way of imagining that one day, I would realize a dream of living in Detroit, the rhythm and blues capitol of the world, about an hour from Michigan State University and the University of Michigan, where some of the greatest college athletes were displaying their talents. So much history and so many stories. Growing up in Oklahoma, the encyclopedia helped to supply some knowledge of what Detroit might have been like here in the 60's…but as Marvin Gaye and Tammi Terrell told us…"Ain't nothing like the real thing, baby" and I agree. Many historians can offer up a glimpse, but they are limited in their view, and we can only hope what we are being told is the truth.

Going toe to toe with Thomas "Hitman" Hearns...with a microphone.

Driving Aretha Franklin on "The Freeway Of Love" in the pink Cadillac. A memory that will never end!

During his seven years with the Detroit Tigers, Cecil Fielder averaged 35 home runs and 108 runs batted in. He demanded my attention.

CHAPTER 12

The Black 14 - The Lies, Like the Story, Will Not Die

HISTORY, MINUS THE TRUTH IS what? The figment of someone's imagination? Possibly at worst a fabrication, an attempt to "spin" reality into a fictional story or situation that doesn't even resemble what actually happened.

My mind raced along those corridors when I discovered the late Dr. William D. Carlson's reminiscence of the Black 14 incident, published in the University of Wyoming's website, uwyo.edu almost 30 years later. The school's former president made some unbelievable assertions in a chapter he labeled, "Athletics' Challenges." There were many claims by Dr. Carlson, who passed away in 2003 that were absolutely false. We never told Head Coach Lloyd Eaton that we planned to wear black armbands while competing against Brigham Young University... or not play. That never happened! Again, Eaton didn't give us a chance to talk when we met with him, prior to us being kicked off the team. But Carlson claims we demanded armbands as a prerequisite to taking the field against BYU.

The Wyoming coaches did not agree to reinstate us if we did not wear the black armbands in protest against BYU, as Carlson says. He also said he and the university helped us to transfer to other schools, and cited Tony McGee and his relocating to Southern University in Baton Rouge, Louisiana as an example. Again, not true. Tony and I ended up at Bishop College in Dallas, thanks to Robert Mayes, my former defensive coach at Booker T. Washington high school.

There were no "hard core" members who controlled the group, and we were not intimidated by the Black Panthers while attempting to reach an amicable resolution with the university, which is what Dr. Carlson would have you believe. The person who stood in the way of resolving our impasse was the one who created it…at the time Lloyd Eaton "owned" Wyoming. No one dared to challenge him. Not the university president…not even the governor. The vast majority of the state, including the attorney general, allied with Eaton, until a year after our dismissal, and a one win and nine loss season, he was fired.

In the August, 2018, edition of the *Wyoming Lawyer* magazine, Richard J. Barrett, special counsel to Wyoming Governor Matt Mead, wrote an item he said was based on his father's 1996 article in the Annals of Wyoming, "The Black 14: Williams v. Eaton, a Personal Recollection" and his detailed conversations with his father during the forty-two years between the Black 14 incident and his death in 2011. Barrett's father, James E. Barrett, was Wyoming's Attorney General in 1969 and the son of Wyoming's 21st Governor, Frank A. Barrett.

James E. Barrett went on to become a judge on the U.S. Court of Appeals, Tenth Circuit. He defended Wyoming, the university, and trustees in our court case, Williams v. Eaton, detailed earlier in this book. Richard J. Barrett's account of what happened to us contained numerous inaccuracies: that during a meeting with UW President William Carlson and Wyoming Governor Stanley Hathaway, we insisted on wearing our black armbands during the game with BYU. We said no such thing. He claimed that four or five of us indicated that regardless of the BYU game, we would not return to the football team. Again it didn't happen. That's simply not true!

I could go on detailing these untruths, but as I mentioned earlier, they were numerous. I did however, contact the Editor in Chief of the Wyoming Lawyer magazine and in the 300 words I was limited to, responded to the article and its assertions:

MY REBUTTAL TO BARRETT
Editor in Chief, Wyoming Lawyer Magazine:

My name is Jay (Jerry) Berry. I am one of the Black 14, and was there in 1969, forced to listen to Lloyd Eaton's racially infused tirade and then be discarded like yesterday's garbage. None of us were allowed to say a single word. For the last 49 years I have tried to dispel lies and inaccuracies, like the ones that appeared in Richard J. Barrett's Black 14 Revisited article.

In Mr. Barrett's account, according to conversations he had with his late father (neither of whom were at the meeting): (1) We met with Coach Eaton with most of the White players; (2) We made remarks during that meeting; (3) One of the players attempted to throw his playbook at Eaton's feet and unintentionally struck the coach in his face and cut his lip; (4) We told Governor Hathaway that we insisted on wearing the black armbands during the BYU game; and (5) None of us indicated we would return to the team if Eaton remained the head coach. These are just a few of the inaccuracies. They simply didn't happen!

Consider this: Why would I, as a 19 year-old student athlete who was enjoying an incredible season personally on a highly ranked team, put everything in jeopardy because of someone else's religious beliefs? Why would I, who knew nothing about the Mormon religion before enrolling at the University of Wyoming, and who as a freshman, seriously entertained an offer to spend Christmas with a Mormon teammate (Cheyenne attorney Wally Stock)...suddenly feel so differently?

I wouldn't! I wanted to ask my coach some questions and was kicked off the team because of it! I was willing to risk personal injury, brain damage and at the worst, death...to proudly wear the Brown & Gold.

Will I get a response from Richard J. Barrett? What would it contain? More inaccuracies or just blatant lies? I really don't know. But this I do know: to allow these continued false recollections go unchecked would be morally wrong, and betray me and the other members of the Black 14. We didn't break any laws by asking to speak to our coach. We weren't demanding anything…or threatening anyone. But by the actions taken against us, it is painfully obvious that freedom of speech, the right to express opinions without censorship or restraint as guaranteed by the United States Constitution, in our case, is sadly make-believe and fantasy in Wyoming.

Roughly 50 years to the date when all 14 Black football players were kicked off an undefeated team, I have received no official apology and certainly no reparations from the state of Wyoming or its university. Our transgression? Wearing black armbands while meeting with our Head Coach Lloyd Eaton. A meeting in which we weren't allowed to speak. In his mind, he had been defied and we would pay!

Unfortunately, injustices of all types will remain a part of our lives, but so will the battles to right these wrongs. Count me among those in the latter group. I fight because, although naïve in the ways of men and women, I know through almighty God, nothing is impossible. I'm strengthened by His word, emboldened by His promises, and wiser because of my lifetime of experiences with Him guiding my way!

From the outhouse…to a life I could never have imagined. Who knew? God did and I am forever thankful! As they say in the biz, "That's a wrap!"

Looking back on an unimaginable life...one I still can't believe.

ACKNOWLEDGEMENTS

While I was privileged to work in some of the best television markets and for some incredible stations, I would be negligent if I didn't thank the Oklahoma Eagle newspaper for giving an opportunity to a young journalist in Tulsa with a column called J's Sports World.

In Detroit, Sam Logan, former publisher of the Michigan Chronicle, extended a hand with another column in The Front Page newspaper after a good word from Karen Dumas. Karen wears many hats, is a true professional, and is someone I am proud to call a friend.

I added radio to my resume when I joined Mildred Gaddis, Tune-Up Man, and John Mason on his WJLB Mason in the Morning show. They were fun, but informative times for sure.

Some years prior to working with Mason and Company I had an opportunity to partner with Tom Joyner on his immensely popular morning show in Chicago. Unfortunately I had to decline his offer. Tom thought I had lost my mind. He said, in only the way he can, "What, you don't like money?"

But I knew those early hours, combined with my late shifts on television, would have led to an early death. I am still kicking and through this book, able to thank everyone who helped to make me a success. My gratitude to all involved!

This memoir, in many abbreviated forms, has been bouncing around in my brain for years. Every move, city, opportunity and each person I have met, helped create another chapter. Often I was told… "You ought to write a book." Over lunch one afternoon with Rickey Hampton, a former reporter with the Flint Journal newspaper, and after his insistence…"Man, you ought to write a book." I finally agreed.

It's been a humbling experience traveling back into my past, reliving my experiences, the unbelievable opportunities and amazing people I have encountered along the way. I have emerged feeling blessed beyond my wildest dreams and realize there are countless individuals who have made this project possible.

Thank you to Jeanne on so many levels, especially where this book is the subject. You are a remarkable person and wife, a friend and supportive soulmate, who has helped provide a loving home and comfortable existence for us. I sincerely thank God for delivering you into my life, enriching it beyond anything I could have imagined.

Thanks also to my daughter Carla, who is a positive motivator and steadfast supporter. She obviously has some of my blood flowing through her, because like me she knows all things are possible through God. Love you Peanut!

Tom and Bethany became a part of my life when I married Jeanne, and my blessings multiplied. Bethany is a thoughtful, intelligent, energizer bunny (much like her mom) who has given me love, reinforcement, assistance and much pride calling her my daughter.

Tom, similar to his sister Bethany, has helped make this book possible (and would be the first to say…"Man, what did I do?") in ways he can't imagine. But his belief in me has been crucial, and reassuring. Thanks man!

A few years ago, Adrienne Vetter, an artist, while working with the Wyoming Arts Council, created a mural of the Black 14 on a building in Laramie, Wyoming. She learned of our story from her mom, who was fresh out of high school when we were kicked off the University of Wyoming football team in 1969. This obviously made an impression on both of them, and they have made an everlasting impression on me. Thank you Adrienne for helping to keep our story relevant five decades later.

Special thanks also to Scott Rogers of Ulmer & Berne LLP, for your efforts, patience, and time in helping me tell my story.

And last, but certainly not least, I probably would still be struggling to publish if not for the talents of Jenny Chandler and the team at Elite Authors. I had to kiss some frogs before I found them, and there was certainly no pleasure in that!

ADDITIONAL CREDITS:

FRONT COVER PHOTOS:
  *Howard Cosell photo courtesy of Val Clark
  *Jacques Cousteau photo courtesy of Robert "Bob" Brandon
  *Nettie Mae Stearnes photo courtesy of family of Norman Thomas "Turkey" Stearnes
  *Sparky Anderson photo courtesy of Unknown
  *Aretha Franklin photo courtesy of Video Production Crew
  *Jay Berry intercepting pass photo courtesy of John Henberg Collection and Wyoming State Archives
  *Best in Texas TV photo (also on p. 175) courtesy of Houston Forward Times Newspaper
  *Black 14 mural photo courtesy of Adrienne Vetter

  Page 57. Wyoming football team photo courtesy of University of Wyoming
  Page 57. Football practice photo courtesy of Laramie Boomerang/Peterson
  Page 175. News 8 photo courtesy of KTUL-TV
  Page 176. Ray Miller and Robert "Bob" Brandon photos courtesy of KPRC-TV
  Page 178. Jay Berry Joins Channel 7 Team courtesy of The Chicago Defender
  Page 178. Eyewitness News Advertising courtesy of WLS-TV
  Page 179. Jay Berry's Odyssey Joe LaPointe article courtesy of Detroit Free Press
  Page 206. Thomas Hearns photo courtesy of Jackie Kallen
  Page 207. Cecil Fielder photo courtesy of Detroit Tigers fan
  BACK COVER. Jay Berry photo courtesy of WXYZ-TV

Made in the USA
Middletown, DE
02 August 2019